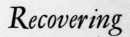

Recovering

Recovering
A Journal

By *May Sarton*

W · W · NORTON & COMPANY · *New York* · *London*

I wish to thank the estate of Margaret Clapp, and Nancy Ellis, Lynn Higgs, Eda
LeShan, Emery Neff, Virginia Russell for permission to quote from personal
letters, William Heyen for permission to quote his poem, *The Field*, and Mary
Stella Edwards for permission to quote her poem, *Thomas Hardy Perhaps*.
Grateful acknowledgment is made to the following: Macmillan Publishing
Co., Inc., for permission to reprint "Two Songs of a Fool," I, from *Collected
Poems* by William Butler Yeats, copyright 1919 by Macmillan Publishing Co.,
Inc., renewed 1947 by Bertha Georgie Yeats; Cresset Press London, for per-
mission to reprint "Reflection" from *A Trophy of Arms* by Ruth Pitter and for
permission to reprint "Epitaph for Everyman" from *On a Calm Shore* by
Francis Cornford. Frontispiece photograph and photographs on pages 39, 99,
136, 172, 215, 223, 235, and 247 are by Beverly Hallam; page 63 by Anne
Woodson; page 129 by B. A. Robidoux; and page 147 by Charles de Wilde. The
pictures on pages 23 and 201 are from *Writers in Residence* (Viking Penguin
Inc.), copyright 1980 Glynne Robinson Betts.

Library of Congress Cataloging in Publication Data
Sarton, May, 1912–
    Recovering: a journal.
    1. Sarton, May 1912–   —Biography.
2. Authors, American—20th century—Biography.
I. Title.
PS3537.A832Z524   1980   818'.5203 [B]   80–15155

ISBN 0-393-30339-X

W. W. Norton & Company, Inc.
500 Fifth Avenue, New York, N.Y. 10110
W. W. Norton & Company, Ltd.
37 Great Russell Street, London WC1B 3NU

1 2 3 4 5 6 7 8 9 0

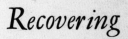

Recovering

Thursday, December 28th, 1978

I HAD THOUGHT not to begin a new journal until I am seventy, four years from now, but perhaps the time has come to sort myself out, and see whether I can restore a sense of meaning and continuity to my life by this familiar means.

Also I need to commemorate with something better than tears my long companionship with Judy that began thirty-five years ago in Santa Fe and ended on Christmas Day. Our last Christmas together; it was a fiasco. I wasn't feeling well and had a low fever when I went to fetch her on Christmas Eve at the Walden Nursing Home where she has been for seven years. I had been warned that she had changed for the worse in her slow progress toward complete senility, but I hoped that after twenty-four hours with me here, she would begin to relate again. That is the way it has been for the last few years and when she was here for her eightieth birthday in September, we did have a few moments of communion.

The furies have been attentive these past months and they must have worked quite hard to bring about all that took place on Christmas morning. There had been a wild gale of wind and rain all night, and when I woke at six in the dark, Tamas suddenly threw up all over the bed. (He has only done this once before.) When I tried to put on the light I realized that the electricity had gone off—no heat, no light, no stove. Luckily I knew where I had a battery-powered lamp and it worked, so I was able to take off the

sheets from my bed and remake it. Then I crept into it
feeling sick and dreading the day ahead. I got up at half
past seven and went in to Judy's room to wake her, and
had to change her sheets. I got her up into a clean night-
gown and settled her in my bed while I went down to see
what could be done about breakfast. I had no fever but
everything seemed an enormous effort as though I were
swimming under water. I did find the sterno and got some
water started. It took nearly half an hour to heat enough
for two cups of tea and we had that and cold cereal for our
breakfast.

Over the years we have always opened our stockings
in bed but Judy no longer enjoys opening presents so I had
given up on stockings and brought up a present from
faithful Emily Huntington for her to unwrap. She showed
no interest in an elegant pair of gray slacks after refusing
to unwrap the package. It was "downhill all the way," and
I began to wonder how I was going to manage. I made
fires in both fireplaces downstairs and got Judy dressed in
a warm sweater and slacks and settled her in an armchair
with a rug over her knees beside the fire in the library.
But she was very restless and was soon up, moving around
in the curious shuffle that has replaced walking now. She
never once looked at the tree, poignantly beautiful this
year, and—as it has been for thirty years—decorated with
the many ornaments we have collected together.

It is often a small thing that shatters hope. For me it
came when a male pheasant appeared close to the porch
window—such a dazzling sight in all the gloom that I
called out, "Come Judy, come quickly!" She didn't come,
of course. I found her shuffling about in the library and by
the time I had dragged her to the window, the pheasant
was out of sight. At that moment I knew that Judy had

gone beyond where being with me in this house means anything.

And slowly, after the light and heat came on at eleven and after I had cooked the duck and given her her dinner (I felt nauseated and couldn't eat myself), I came to the decision to take her back that very afternoon. Luckily we had carols all the way on the car radio and a dramatic sky as sun broke through in great slashes from under purple and black clouds. That drive *was* Christmas this year.

Now I am more alone than ever before, for as long as Judy was here at least for the holidays, and even though only *partially* here, as long as I could recreate for a few days or hours a little of the old magic Christmases at 139 Oxford Street and then at 14 Wright Street in Cambridge, I still had family. Better than that, for families are often not in perfect communion, and Judy and I for over thirty years have been able to rest on a foundation of wordless understanding. There is no one now with whom I can feel perfectly "at home" in just the way I did with Judy. She knew me, warts and all, and had long ago accepted me, warts and all, as I had her, for this was a true love.

Now it has become the past, a beneficent past. I have before me a delightful photograph of Judy and me, both smiling, on the dock at Greenings Island as we were about to embark for the shore after our last stay there with Anne Thorp. As Judy became old, we gave up on permanents; her hair is a smooth white cap like a boy's and makes me remember that her friends at Smith College used to call her Mowgli.

A Christmas strangely without tenderness. Or rather with only the tenderness of strangers, for there have been nourishing letters about *A Reckoning* and several also begging me to do another journal by the sea. "It is as if they are a special gift to help in the healing process in my life . . . you have been a dear friend to me." Is there anyone, I sometimes wonder, who is not wounded and in the process of healing?

For me it is always poetry that comes as the healer and it was a moment of illumination when I came across this one by William Heyen in the December issue of *Poetry*

The Field

Each Christmas Eve, outside alone
in a field of the black sheen of snow,
I close my eyes: soon
that script appears again, roots

of the dead elms and chestnuts
underground, aglow.
The word was never lost,
my friends—as if we didn't know.

Friday, December 29th

THE ATTACK of flu on Christmas Eve has now turned into what my father would have called "the worst cold I ever had." His only infirmity until late in his life was the recurrence of head colds and, having forgotten the last one, he was each time convinced that the present one was the worst. It's amazing how quickly we forget pain after it is over, part no doubt of what seems an infinite capacity for renewal, those roots "underground, aglow" that Heyen speaks of in his poem.

Colette says "I believe that there are more urgent and honorable occupations than that incomparable waste of time we call suffering." She means, I deduce, indulgence, what the French have a phrase for, *délectation morose,* the tendency to love one's own pain and to wallow in it.

On the other hand the only way through pain, and I am thinking of mental anguish of which I have had rather too much this past year, is to go through it, to absorb, probe, understand exactly what it is and what it means. To close the door on pain is to miss the chance for growth, isn't it? Nothing that happens to us, even the most terrible shock, is unusable, and everything has somehow to be built into the fabric of the personality, just as food has to be built in.

For me the moral dilemma this past year has been how to make peace with the unacceptable—where compromise is part of wisdom and where, on the other hand, what my old friend Pauline Prince calls "your thirst for the absolute" seems the commanding necessity. In human relations at least there cannot be an absolute and to demand it is to be a wrecker as I have sometimes been. So the word that has run through these past months has been "accept, accept." How unregenerate I feel when I rebel, as I do most of the time, against accepting!

The light these December mornings has a rather special quality; austere, cold as it is, it has amplitude, a spacious austerity. I live with a wide semi-circle of horizon over and beyond the bare field. Snow would make it richer, but in my mood at present, I rest on the cold gray sea. And wait for the sun's rays to catch a tiny prism Karen Saum hung in my bedroom window, wait for that sudden flame, first crimson then sometimes a flash of blue, startlingly alive.

Saturday, December 30th

YESTERDAY I FELT quite ill and afraid of going out into the
icy air to walk Tamas, so what a marvelous happening
when Karen Saum called from Kittery on her way home
—she is hoping to do a documentary video tape on my life
here and wanted to tell me about her interviews in Washington about raising the money for this. She stopped by,
walked Tamas, got the mail for me while I made her a
roast beef sandwich, and the whole color of life came back
like a flush on a wan cheek. She had some amazing stories
to tell about mis-directions in the bureaucracy that led
her, by chance, to the wrong floor, to the wrong room, to
an interested and helpful person. It makes me laugh to
think how chancy life is, how anything may happen at any
moment, just as her unexpected visit changed the day for
me.

I have to admit that this is an acutely lonely Christmas
week, and to realize as I think about it, that for most
people Christmas is rather an ordeal; what we do not have
looms a great deal larger than what we do have. The price
of family life (what we all dream of at Christmas) is very
high too, and full of self-discipline and pain. Even feeling
rather ill, even having to say goodbye to Judy and our life
together, even recovering from some rather severe blows
in the last two months, I also have to admit that I love my
life and that when I am alone here, the excitement inside
me is very great and often fruitful, that the animals pro-

vide a certain sweet companionship I treasure, and that in essence it is not a wasteful life. It is a life that has meaning and thrust even on the worst of days.

I'm glad I decided to begin a journal again. It is a way of sorting myself out, that self that has been too dispersed for too long, partly because of the long weeks in November when I was away on poetry readings and book signings, flying off in a hundred directions, meeting old friends for a few concentrated hours, responding on too many levels. Since September the only writing I have done is answering letters; the responsive nerve wears out after months of this.

So here I am again, renewing acquaintance with my self.

"A Christmas without tenderness," I wrote two days ago. And since then I have been sent back by that word to Jean Dominique, to her poems, and to the exquisite tenderness, humor, and loving grace with which she managed to live and to go on loving to the very end. Mothers are very good at tenderness, and it is, no doubt, the mothering part of us that can give it, and the child part of us that longs to feel it in the atmosphere. For me it is associated with Europe, with fine distinctions between it and sentimentality, for one thing. Sentimentality is the debasing of feeling by making it less than itself; it is also trite, the overused easy way of diminishing feeling into indistinct mawkishness, and often the clothing of feeling in cheap clothes, cheap language. Whereas true tenderness makes us know we are cherished—simply in a droll pet name, for example. It often expresses itself through humor.

I am starved for tenderness and that is what is the matter with me and has been the matter with me for months.

Sunday, December 31st

TENDERNESS is the grace of the heart, as style is the grace
of the mind, I decided when I couldn't sleep last night.
Both have something to do with quality, the quality of
feeling, the quality of reasoning.

The last day of what has been an uneasy and painful
year for me. I look forward to dawn tomorrow and, as the
days get longer, to begin to feel my way into renascence.
It is not strange though it is mysterious that our "New
Year" comes at the darkest time in the seasonal cycle.
When there is personal darkness, when there is pain to be
overcome, when we are forced to renew ourselves against
all the odds, the psychic energy required simply to survive has tremendous force, as great as that of a bulb push-
ing up through icy ground in spring, so after the overcoming, there is extra energy, a flood of energy that can go
into creation. This morning I began a short novel that has
been haunting me for months, since last summer, in fact.

Monday, January 1st, 1979

I HEAR they have bitter cold and deep snow in England as well as a foot and a half in Chicago, while here on the coast it is as warm as April with a gentle rain falling. This year, this new year, it is fitting, for me at any rate, that it opens not with a clash of cymbals but with the gentle soundless rain. For as I look back on the disasters of 1978 I perceive that my fault has been to hope too much, to allow myself to be swept on an inner trajectory too swift and too sure of itself. Pauline Prince in a recent letter that helped me a lot used the image of Icarus when she spoke of my thirst for the absolute—I had somehow made up my mind that *A Reckoning* would do well enough to give me a year off. More, that it would be a real success, a critical success. That was not to be. And I had hoped to feel solid ground under my feet as far as is possible in a passionate human relationship. That, too, has proved to be an illusion, so I am back where I started in a rather complete isolation both as a professional writer and as a woman. And what I have been doing this past week—and what keeping a journal again is helping me to do—is to make my peace with solitude once more, and to come back to work without ambition, for the joy of it, Icarus who tried to reach the sun, falling back to the earth.

I'm on a great reading jag, too . . . the Virginia Woolf biography by Phyllis Rose. In spite of the plethora of material about Woolf, including her own letters and journals,

I find it illuminating. The E. M. Forster biography is there by my bed and there are several pots of honey waiting to be devoured of the same ilk, Spender's thoughts on the thirties for one. I am reading poetry again and playing records, especially these days Bruckner's Ninth Symphony, sent me by a monk sometime ago.

It is a time of turning back to roots, to the great influences, going back in order to draw strength from the deep sources. I count among them Ruth Pitter and just now opened to this poem from *A Trophy Of Arms,* (The Cresset Press, 1937).

Reflection

> The winter falls and the winds groan;
> God shall remain though I be gone.
> I loved my life, I desired joy;
> This was a fault, this was a toy.
> An immortality I had
> When I was young; then was I glad;
> In summertime I felt no rue
> For what the certain frost would do.
> Ah bitter beauty, thou art delusion,
> Though true enough I know to be
> The horror and the dire confusion
> That a clear vision shows to me.
> Enough; give me my proven mail,
> My arms of faith that cannot fail:
> I cleave the chaos and prevail.

Now on this first day of a New Year, I am in a quiet way blooming. And this year, no more wild hopes. Then maybe the Furies so present in the last two months will go elsewhere.

Tuesday, January 2nd

THE WEATHER is upside down. When I called Karen Buss on New Year's Day to tell her I thought a novella she had sent me was magnificent (and it is!) she told me that down there near Dallas they had spent the whole day clearing up the wreckage of their trees after an ice storm! In Chicago, deep snow, and here on the East Coast, what? Warm rain, soft wet ground! I walked Tamas and Bramble down to the rocks yesterday and stood for minutes watching the long, towering waves sweep in and break, exulting in all that thundering power let loose. Sometimes the un-measured, the unlimited natural powers are what I need, what everyone needs. I am tired of measure, control, doing the right thing. A part of me would like to tear something apart and howl like a wolf!

Yesterday I called Carol Heilbrun who has the most restorative presence on the telephone of anyone I know. I think it is because she laughs in a totally compassionate way at the absurd horrors of life, such as my Christmas, and the laughter makes me laugh too. Laughter and tears, the breakers of tension, and very close really because they are that. I told Carol I was keeping a journal again and she told me to "tell it like it is" about the depression, "bring it out," whereas I have felt a kind of reluctance to do so, because I am determined to begin the new year without an albatross round my neck. But maybe the albatross can only be cut off by facing what it is once and for all.

In November just before reading poems at MacAlaster College in St. Paul, Minnesota, I picked up the first issue of the Sunday *Times* since the strike, and turned eagerly to the review of *A Reckoning*. Rumor had it that at long last this one would be warm, so what I found was shocking, a mean-spirited review by Lore Dickstein, "a freelance writer" who has little understanding of structure and based her review apparently on a lot of *a priori* beliefs about me and my work. She even dragged in a poem, "My Sisters, O My Sisters," written thirty years ago or more and called it a "Lesbian love poem" when in fact, had Miss Dickstein bothered to read it to the end, she would have discovered that it is rather the opposite, a plea that women "Give their greatness back to men" if they are ever to become whole women, and in the first section (which she quotes) that the woman writer no longer has to be "strange" or "isolated."

"Where nothing has to be renounced or given over
In the pure light that shines out from the lover,

In the warm light that brings forth fruit and flower
And that great sanity, that sun, the feminine power."

The poem has no relevance to the novel she is reviewing, which she has misguidedly called a Lesbian novel in disguise.

I had a lot of letters about the review, from all over the country. It made readers who had read the novel angry. And with reason. My favorite was one from Los Angeles that ended "I hope I can write a novel someday that Lore Dickstein will *hate.*"

Every writer is too aware of his own defects, too filled with anxiety about his work, too full of self-doubt to be able blithely to cast aside a bad review. It is a drop of poison and slowly gets into the system, day by day. The

Times has sneered at or attacked every book of mine since
Faithful Are The Wounds—that got a rave and I am ever-
lastingly grateful to Brendan Gill who wrote it—except
Crucial Conversations which Doris Grumbach reviewed
thoughtfully. So the effect of this last public beating was
as bad as it was, I think, because it was cumulative. You
can rise above one or two public humiliations such as this,
but finally after ten or more it gets to you. I felt finished.
I felt that I would not again expose myself to such pain.
I felt like a deer shot down by hunters.

Usually in life one can reply or defend oneself against
attack, but one of the reasons a bad review is hard to take
is that one has to sit still and do nothing.

People say to me, "Why do you care what a nobody
like Dickstein says? You know it isn't true." Here one
must face the practical fact that my livelihood as well as
my talent as a writer are involved. A bad review keeps
readers from buying a book, it is as simple as that. When
a major work near the end of a long life is "wasted" in this
way, it means that the writer must set to at once and
produce another in order to keep afloat financially. I had
set my heart, as I wrote the other day, on a real success
this time, on the cumulative effect of what is now a consid-
erable "oeuvre," as well as the value of this novel in itself.
It hurt that the *Times* thought so little of me as to give the
book to a nobody.

I had some reason to hope this time. One of the first
letters that came in on this book was from Eda LeShan
and it meant a great deal to me because this was word
from the horse's mouth. She says in part:

I have been reading *A Reckoning* for about three days during
which time I had a great many appointments and assignments,
but the reality of my days had nothing to do with any of it—my

only absorption was following a dying woman's quest for identity.

"I am convinced that your book is the most important statement about the experience of dying since Tolstoy's *Death of Ivan Illych.* It is a subject about which my husband and I know a good deal—he especially, since he worked on a research project for about twenty years in which he worked with the dying, constantly.

"He is a research psychologist, and his interest stemmed from a feeling that cancer was, under some circumstances, a psychosomatic disease having to do with a fairly specific personality complex and certain life experiences—most of all a sense of despair about not having lived one's own life. In his work with terminal cancer patients (psychotherapy) the search was always to help the person find his or her own authenticity, sense of personal identity—and this was important and necessary, no matter what the outcome. What you have done so magnificently as an artist, he struggled to do through scientific research —but we always knew the artist's vision was clearer, more necessary and ultimately all that counted.

Wednesday, January 3rd

IT WAS NOT a good idea to go back to all that. But at least today we have seasonal weather. Yesterday there was darkness, heavy rain, temperature around 50 degrees. Now it is 20 and the sun shines over the muddy gray field. The trouble is that my flu is now in the coughing stage. I feel infected and low in energy. It is a new year but I haven't caught hold of it yet, still dangling uncomfortably

over the pit of depression. In this state I find making decisions hard . . . I had to decide about two lectures in California in April. I'll be in the Midwest at the end of March at Wabash and Olivet, so it would make sense to go out then, but I am reluctant before the huge effort involved. And I finally called the dear girl who has taken it on herself to try to get me out there, to ask for time. I refused one of the two, which involved an immediate decision on my part. The other, at San Francisco State College would be an interesting audience and they have wanted me to come before. So maybe I'll go out anyway, though the fee won't even pay the flight.

For a few days just after Christmas I was beginning to feel at home in myself, and to realize again the immense joys of having time to think, to be quiet, to live along in a sedate routine, that routine that for me releases the imagination, a quiet earth but a quiet earth under wild tumultuous skies . . . Now the pressures begin again. The battle begins again for an hour or two at my desk when I can "let go," let go the guilt over the un-answered, the un-responded to, and open the door into the sub-conscious. The novella moves slowly because I haven't the psychic energy to make that primary leap, when everything still has to be imagined and created. Too bad about the flu. It is holding me back.

Thursday, January 4th

IT'S EXHILARATINGLY COLD for a change, cold and bright.
There are moments of pure joy. Yesterday when I got up
from my nap and a long think, and went down, there were
three purple finches at the feeder! So far, this winter has
been a sparse one for birds. Five or six chickadees, a nut-
hatch, and a pair of downy woodpeckers are about it. No
jays, which is strange. Ann Woodson told me the Audubon
people say there are few birds anywhere this fall (in this
area anyway). The deer, for the first time since I've been
here, come right up to the terrace and have chewed up
nearly all the euonymus bushes, kept cut in round shapes
by Raymond. They have also eaten most of the yew in
several places. Ann told me it is because there are no
acorns this year—the deer are starving. Such things are a
little scary. Why are there no acorns? Why are there no
birds?

So it was a particularly enlivening moment yesterday
when I saw the purple finches. Another joy these days is
to pick up the small sculpture Barbara made for me for
Christmas of a hibernating chipmunk. It lies on a piece of
circular roughened rock that has been smoothed around
inside and the chipmunk itself makes a perfect circle nose
to tail, in this sculptured nest. Holding it in my hand,
heavy, round and smooth, is a peace-inducing pleasure.

But the early morning is the time of purest joy. As the
sun rises it shines through the brilliant azaleas and cycla-

men in the plant window like a Hosannah. That starts the day off with a lift.

Then when I take my breakfast up again to bed and lie there in my spacious bedroom, thinking about the day ahead, soaking in the light as it touches the plain wood of the bureau and lovely wide-framed mirror above it that Judy gave me, touches the photograph of Bel-Gazou, Bramble's brother, the most loveable cat I ever had, I am thankful to be here, thankful for the silence. It is so silent! Sometimes I don't even hear the ocean.

There is still an undertow of depression. The "bad thoughts" come creeping in through every undefended crevice of my consciousness. Then it is time to get up, come up here to my study, and get to work. That is the only valid medicine against the flu, old age, depression— so here I am.

Friday, January 5th

THE WORST THING right now is that I no longer have any distant hopes, anything ahead that I look forward to with a leap of the heart. What I have lost this past year is the sense of a destiny, the belief that what I have to offer as a human being in love or as a writer with a great deal of published work behind her, is worthy . . . which means worth all the struggle and pain that has gone both into love and work. In naked terms, I simply feel a failure. Too old to hope that things will ever get any better. I have been "put down" in such brutal ways that recovery is only possible by dogged self-discipline. And it is not true recovery, it is simply not committing suicide, keeping alive, using the tools I have at hand, being a writer because that skill is the only one I have at my command. I still cannot "recover" from the things that have happened last year.

A trajectory, the sense I had of myself and my own powers, has been broken.

Saturday, January 6th

AFTER BREAKFAST this morning I read Alexander Eliot's portrait of Berenson in the latest *Smithsonian*. It brought back vivid memories of the week I spent there when the Murdocks were Harvard's managers there after B.B.'s death, a house still full of a presence, and of a life that had demanded hours of solitude and contemplation and hours of intelligent conversation. I was on my way back from celebrating my fiftieth birthday by going to Japan, India, and Greece, climbing the Acropolis on the day itself, May 3rd. Never shall I forget the clarity of the air after the soupy air of Bombay. The day before yesterday Cronkite showed the dismal results of industrialization, the devastating havoc of smog on the sculptures of the Acropolis, so I saw it just in time.

I Tatti was the perfect place as a "retreat" after taking in so much in three overwhelming months of travel alone. The effect on me was like that of music, a gathering together and a release at the same time. So I read this quotation from B.B.'s *Sketch for a Self Portrait* this

morning with absolute recognition, "From childhood on
I have had the dream of life lived as a sacrament . . . The
dream implied taking life ritually as something holy."

To do this one must, perhaps, be serving something
greater than oneself. And at his best Berenson served by
making thousands of people begin to see what he saw in
a painting or in any work of art. With nothing behind him
to help, this exquisite creature fashioned himself to an
ideal, became what he had chosen to be. How rare.

Monday, January 8th

POURING RAIN TODAY and all last night. I wonder
whether Huldah, who is coming tonight, will be able to
get out, for in New Hampshire it must be heavy snow, a
foot or more. I had hoped for good weather.

I hated to finish Robert Phelps' compendium on Colette, *Belles Saisons,* last night. I felt like a bear who has
finished a pot of honey and licks and licks at the edges for
a last taste.

I saw Colette just once. Lugné-Poë had taken me to a
first night (I have forgotten the play entirely) and there in
the lobby was Colette, who looked at first like a dwarf, she
was so short and stocky, with that mass of flaming hair and
her slanting piercing eyes looking out of a mask, for she
wore a great deal of makeup, Lugné took me over to meet
her and I felt her penetrating gaze "take me in" as though
she had read the whole book in a second, and then was not
interested.

Last night I marked two sentences, two lessons if you will. When beginning a new novel she wrote Francis Carco, "It's terrible to think as I do every time I begin a book, that I no longer have, and never have had, any talent." And later, in accepting her election to The Royal Academy of French Letters in Belgium, "the only virtue on which I pride myself is my self-doubt. If every day I find myself more circumspect toward my work, and more uncertain as to whether I should continue, my only self-assurance comes from my fear itself. For when a writer loses his self-doubt, the time has come to lay aside his pen."

She has not been read as she should be in the United States, though she has become a legend as a personality, and the reason may be that she is nearly untranslatable. The language, the style itself, is French. Rilke is the only other writer who appears to lose as much in translation.

How does one translate, for instance, the title of her husband Goudeket's wonderful book about her, *Près de Colette?* "Near Colette" doesn't work at all. "Close to Colette" is not it either. For in that "près de" there is homage, the loving and selfless observer, for whom the phrase "close to" would have seemed like boasting.

Her genius was in finding the exact word, especially the exact word for a sensation, the texture of a flower, the feel of a peach in the hand, and in one marvelous passage in *Le Fanal Bleu* (I believe it is there, one of her last autobiographical books anyway), the difference in taste between oranges, from Haifa, from Seville, from Greece, from the South of France. The art of making exquisite distinctions. Nothing is blurred or wrapped up in a cliché. It is all fresh. So it is not surprising that she sat for a half hour sometimes over a single adjective. How I admire that patience, the patience of a cat at a mousehole!

And of course what she understood, better than anyone perhaps, is the pathos of sensuality. She is never
coarse and never overtly sexual because there is always
the implicit understanding of the poignance in a caress.

Thursday, January 11th

TEMPERATURE ZERO this morning. And at long last we
are promised snow this weekend. Never have I known a
winter where there has been so little snow by mid-Janu-
ary. I long for the snow silence and the snow dazzle and
the blue sea beyond an ermine instead of a soggy pale
brown foreground of field.

The house feels desolate without Huldah in it and the
two big collies, Scottie carried in and out of the car on a
mattress where she has lain for the past three months
since she was hit by a truck last autumn. Will she ever
walk again? It is moving to see such an act of faith and love
as Huldah has shown, the endless lifting and cleaning up,
and the unfailing tenderness. What is so touching about a
sick animal is the patience and lack of self-pity, and of
course the total dependence on human care.

The American ethos permits a show of feeling toward
animals but often makes people censor a show of feeling
toward human beings. Is it the fear of loss? Or is it the idea
that to show feeling, and especially to weep, is a sign of
weakness?

I ask these questions today, as I have often before, in
the light of a piece that appeared the other day in the

Times by Benjamin Blech, a rabbi in Oceanside, N.Y. (*New York Times,* Sunday, December 31, 1978). He says:

> What is it about our value system that makes crying a crime and the show of feelings the most shameful failing?
>   I cannot be sure of the cause. But I know that Kierkegaard was right: what our age lacks is not reflection but passion—and we pay the price in incalculable pain and suffering.

Probably we all justify ourselves, our natures I mean to say, by a philosophical concept. I am a very open person, feel intensely and am able to show feeling, cry a lot (Blech's title, by the way, is "Cry, Please Cry") and there is no doubt that such a nature is suspect. The Puritan ethic, and we are all steeped in it in the USA, emphasized self-control as the highest virtue. Feeling is anarchic, breaks down barriers, and that can be dangerous. Weeping is for women and means weakness, lack of self-respect; for self-respect implies control, even more, self-sufficiency. Tears are almost always a cry for help.

Blech goes on to say:

> It is the tragedy of our times that we consider nature's way of healing a weakness, even as we continue to confuse emotion with immaturity . . . Why must the ideal response of human behavior be "cool" when the warmth of emotional commitment best expresses the language of love and concern?

And later Blech quotes Whitehead:

> Intellect is to emotion as our clothes are to our bodies; we could not very well have civilized life without clothes, but we would be in a poor way if we had only clothes without bodies.

And Blech continues:

> What I mourn in our age is the unnatural contempt
> for natural manifestations of emotion . . . And that is
> why I am not ashamed to admit that whenever I see
> models of self-control I weep for them.

Maybe one has to be strongenough to admit one's
need, to become fully human.

Friday, January 12th

BECAUSE I LIVE ALONE and have for the past twenty
years, I write from there. But I am becoming aware these
days that of the two kinds of people who read me with the
greatest interest—the first, people who live alone because
they are widows, people to whom solitude has "happened," and the second, young people who have not yet
made a commitment to life either in work or love—to the
latter I may present a role model that is dangerous rather
than helpful. I have come to represent the life of solitude
as, per se, a valid choice as against marriage or even productive work. Maybe it is true that there are two times in
life when solitude can be productive, when one is twenty
and again after sixty. But of the two only in the former is
solitude a choice. And in the former it is almost bound to
be a temporary choice, for life is going to move in in all
probability and change the course.

If one does choose solitude it must be for a purpose
other than mere self-seeking; the search for "identity" is
a fashionable concept these days, but sometimes at least

it looks like pure self-indulgence. How does one find one's identity? My answer would be through work and through love, and both imply giving rather than getting. Each requires discipline, self-mastery, and a kind of selflessness, and they are each lifetime challenges. Who writes a perfect masterpiece or is a perfect lover? I have spent the morning answering a long letter from a young woman still in college, one of many others I have received in the last year or so, who looks on my way of living as far easier than it is, and probably happier than it is, as against her mother's life which seems to her impossible and unfulfilling! What follows is my answer:

Dear—————

You have to remember as you sort things out that I did not begin to live alone until I was 45 and went to Nelson *(Plant Dreaming Deep)*. Agreed that human relationships are often painful, always maybe collisions, but through them we grow. How do we grow otherwise? You yourself say in this letter, "It is in my times alone that I straighten things out" . . . exactly. But there would be nothing to straighten out if you had no relationships.

You imply that what you want is "love" as a sideline and "solitude" as the main current. I don't see this as possible, for love without commitment is pretty cheap. This is where marriage comes in. I read you as terribly afraid of being "caught" . . . and people who marry simply because they want marriage do often find themselves caught. It looks to me as though you had never loved a man enough to want to marry him, and it's as simple as that. When you do, and I hope you will, there won't be any argument. And then, wouldn't you want children?

There has to be commitment somewhere or life has no meaning. Can one be committed simply to oneself? I think not. From the time I was 30 and had some proof that there was a real talent at work, I committed myself to the art of writing, wanted to serve that art with all I could give it. But in this letter at least I do not see that you have a *vocation* powerful enough in its pull to justify a life of solitude . . . or to fill that life with enough real challenge and discipline to justify it.

You are so young, dear . . . .! You have time to feel your way. No one would ask you to make final decisions now. "Let life do it," Louise Bogan used to say to me. But don't shut life out, or the possibilities of marriage as one of the options open to you.

I myself feel excruciatingly deprived and, yes, often lonely because there is no "central person" in my life now. But I do have work to do and a constant response to it that makes me feel that life has meaning. My animals, flowers in the plant window, the sunrise over the sea are all consolations for that empty feeling—but they could never feel like the *whole of life*.

I understand well that you are drawn to women especially at your age, it is so much easier in every way to have a woman lover than a man lover. And maybe it is not a bad way to begin to understand about love . . . to come to terms with your sensual self, to come to love your body and appreciate all it can feel and give you and give someone else. The danger is that the love of another woman is sometimes a kind of narcissism. I do not see it as as fulfilling in the long run as marriage. I know you don't want to hear this but I must be honest with you. I want my influence not to narrow my young friends down, but to open the path for them . . . Lesbian relations have one serious defect. They rarely last. And one reason they don't last is because it is very easy to break up . . . and another reason is that Lesbians don't have children. From what I have observed around me and in my own life, in a Lesbian couple if it does last, one member takes on most of the obligations of being a wife. So it *is* marriage, in a way, but with none of the supports (social, even job supports) that a marriage gives.

My only advice really is to go ahead and do whatever you feel deeply . . . and maybe you need a year alone at some point, maybe after college. If you truly love a woman then be with her and make a life with her. But an uncommitted life, a life of pure self-indulgence, just won't work because it cannot feed your deep hungers . . . even that hunger "to be with myself, that relationship I find most satisfying."

I don't know whether you have read my book *A World of Light* but in it I quote my father as saying in his journal, "It is clear to me that the main purpose of a man's life is to give others what is in him. Such a matter is not a question of selfishness or unselfishness. Mozart was probably rather selfish in a childish way, but he gave the world what was in him (he could not help it) and *what* a gift.

"We only have what we are, and we only have what we give. That is, we only have what we are, but on condition that we give all that is in us."

I read your letter with the greatest interest and gratitude . . . but what I missed in it was any idea of "giving." Is this something you might think about now?

Saturday, January 13th

AT LAST IT IS SNOWING, the enclosed white world I have longed for, for it is the first real snow this winter. This afternoon I have been making Coq au Vin for Jo Neilson who is coming for lunch tomorrow. Three weeks ago I was too depressed to make that kind of effort, so it's a good sign, and there is something very cosy about cooking in a snowstorm. I enjoyed it, although it took a lot longer than I had planned on. There are yellow tulips and white iris opening downstairs, and now after dark at five the house is very silent, both Tamas and Bramble curled up asleep, Tamas in his bed downstairs and Bramble up here on the couch, a perfect round with her head tucked into her paws.

While I cooked and brewed, I thought about that girl who hates the idea of being a wife and mother because she sees only too clearly what chores are involved and looks on her mother as a prisoner to be pitied. It is very easy to take that stance these days since so many women who are wives and mothers suffer frustration, God knows. But there are times when I am revolted by the reasons for refusing responsibilities and burdens (as though one could!), for looking upon nurturing as a somewhat contemptible task. The trouble with housework of course is that it is so repetitive. You have only just cleaned up after one meal when it is all to be done again. But these young women appear to forget that every job has its routine side, its frustrations and blank spaces. Students never imagine how many hours their professors are expected to give gladly to writing endless recommendations, or for that matter the sheer hard work that goes into preparing a single lecture. Any meaningful task requires an unholy amount of effort and it is this that people seem more and more unwilling to give.

But there are some who do. I think of Martha Wheelock who is a vegetarian and willingly spends hours cutting vegetables up, makes delicious meals, and says that she can meditate while she does it; and she leads a hectic professional life. There are some who see the sacramental side of cooking and housework. Putting clean sheets on a bed, for instance, in fact making order out of disorder any time anywhere, can be regarded as a sacrament.

Wednesday, January 17th

WINTER HAS FINALLY arrived in its most cruel form here: glare ice. Walking is a scary business and I envy Bramble who takes off across the swamp, now frozen solid, while Tamas and I walk the rutted frozen road. I creep along in my heavy boots with a corrugated sole, and he dashes off into the woods. There are few birds though he did flush a partridge the other day, and the day before yesterday I heard the twittering of a flock of evening grosbeaks though I didn't see them. It is zero when I go down in the morning, and it is at this time of year that the plant window, a glorious jumble of pinks, reds, and whites, azaleas and cyclamen mostly, is a daily blessing as the rising sun shines through all the brilliant petals. The other delightful distraction now is the seed catalogues, an orgy of desires and hopes to ponder and choose among. I still dream of someday successfully growing Meconopsis, the bright blue poppy. "The impossible dream!" Maybe I'll try again this year.

Yesterday Susie and Ed Kenney drove down from China for lunch, and we sat by the fire and caught up on our lives for three rich hours, and ate up the rest of the Coq au Vin, a salad, and some Christmas goodies. I miss the children who are growing up so fast, but we did need a good adult talk this time. And now I hope to get them all four here for a picnic on the rocks this summer. One thing we talked about was how Jamie and Anne are almost laughable exemplars of masculine and feminine natures, in spite of all we are told about these characteristics being formed by society and/or the parents. Not so here. Jamie is a wizard at any engineering task, building toys, and immensely curious about how things work. Ann is totally maternal, has now dressed in diapers two koala bears that hug each other that I gave her, and "puts to bed" innumerable animals and dolls every night, just as I did at her age.

Thursday, January 18th

AT LAST I look out on an ermine field! The whole landscape has become rich and strange since the snow last night. The harsh ice has given way to this opulent softness and we can celebrate the festival of winter when Tamas rolls himself clean, his eyes sparkling with pleasure, and Bramble scoots up trees and dashes into the soft white piles in great excitement.

But I slept badly and feel dull this morning, dreading the effort of getting into the novella, now twenty-one pages long. Of course the first fifty pages are the hardest, when everything has to be invented, the scene itself, the characters, their backgrounds. I do feel some momentum at last, but I always forget how hard the work is, what it asks of one every day for months to lift a book out. And that is partly because there is no immediate necessity to get the adrenalin going . . . I think of Huldah lifting poor Scottie in and out of the car for the past three months,

until Scottie died, a long hard life. But the dog was there, needing her. She did not have to summon some buried part of herself in order to do it—that part was right at the surface. And she had no doubts that she must do it, that it was worth doing. I have been battling a loss of identity as a writer these past months. I feel like a clock that is running down. It is pure self-indulgence to spend time and energy explaining this, instead of getting to work!

Monday, January 22nd

FOR ONCE I had some luck—the weather with a fresh snow of about six inches was perfect last Friday and Saturday when first Karen Saum and her crew came to make the teaser for the video tape interview she is planning, and then on Saturday Martha Wheelock and Marita Simpson to make the teaser for the documentary film interview. I planned the two days consecutively on purpose, as less of an interruption than at two separate times, and it was good luck to have good weather, since yesterday we had, of all things, a deluge of rain for twenty-four hours, about the darkest day I've seen here. I spent it lying around hoping that rest would diminish the severe abdominal pain that has been getting worse since Christmas. It is better today since I can sit and type. Yesterday that was not possible. But I guess I had better see a doctor. Nervous tension is the problem, no doubt.

The cameras were around for six hours each day to get

what was wanted for a ten-minute teaser! How I admired the crews' patience, the endless adjustments of lights and cameras, and the way Karen's three worked together, not a moment's irritation. It was extremely cold both days, just above zero, but fortunately the wind died down for a while, and the next day Marita and Martha got some marvelous shots down on the point. I have not been down because of the ice (the path is glare ice under the snow) but we drove down the Firth's road, and it was thrilling to see the big surf come in and have that long sustained roar in our ears. And it was fun to have these lively young friends of mine around, concentrating on their work. I am not cut out to be a movie actress . . . the endless waiting did create a lot of tension. The first day I used some of the waiting time cooking a rabbit with onions and sour cream, and the second day Martha and Marita stopped for an hour and we sat down to lunch—strawberries they had brought with them and a bottle of Liebfraumilch, so I was able to catch up a little with their lives. But by the time they left as dusk came, I was exhausted, that kind of fatigue when you are too tired to do anything, even rest. It is then that the animals are a help—I lay down on my bed with Tamas and Bramble (they too had had a tiring day with so much happening and so many people around to bark at and to be caressed by) and slowly felt the release from tension.

In a way yesterday was not bad. It must be three or four years since I have been sick enough to "give up." I wrote five letters before ten a.m. and then simply had to lie down. Rain pelting against the windows and a somber darkness in my bedroom, usually so drenched in light. Late in the afternoon I caught *Little Lord Fauntleroy* (with Freddie Bartholomew, *not* Mary Pickford!), the most sentimental of tales, but I was in a lazy sentimental mood myself and I loved it. It brought back dear memories of my mother reading it aloud to me, for one thing. And also of a train journey in England when I was seven or eight and she told me the whole story of *Sarah Crewe,* and we had tea in baskets.

Today the sun is out and I'm back at work—

Thursday, January 25th

THERE IS BIG SURF today after a night of wild wind and rain. As I was getting up the lights went off. It is quite comforting to have Brooks' men here finishing up on installing the washer-dryer I have at last decided to put in. How deeply satisfying a real wild storm such as this is to some violent part of oneself that is let out by it, or met by it—the irrational powers set loose. I was awake for half the night thinking. . . .

There has been a hiatus because I drove down to Wellesley yesterday to see how Eleanor Blair is getting on. She broke her hip three weeks ago, and, proving again her valiance and her strength, got back home with a walker two and a half weeks after the operation. She is alone, though with attentive neighbors and friends to do errands, and 'meals on wheels' delivered for a week or so. She had been persuaded to have a practical nurse for a few hours a day, but after a few days, had learned to manage and felt it would be an irritation rather than a help. In this I believe she is right. The important thing (due also to failing eyesight) is to know where every chair and object in her dear little house is. The hospital has been very helpful, getting a hospital bed in, and helping her work things out.

There she was when I pushed open the door, bright as a robin, sitting surrounded by flowers and plants in her wing chair in a charming dressing gown. I kept thinking of a line from an old poem of mine "further limitations release deeper powers." Well into her eighties, she still takes calamity as a challenge, flourishes on her own sense of independence and of "being able to manage" against the odds. For who would dream that she could be alone in her house under these circumstances?

Lovely to see Cindy, her fluffy gray cat curled up asleep on the hospital bed!

She has been such a good neighbor herself that it is satisfying to see the neighborhood rallying around her now, for instance a boy shovelling the snow from her drive all on his own and never a word said.

Friday, January 26th

THE LONG POUNDING of rain, wind, and wet snow has ended after twenty-four hours of glorious surf, but also of enervating wind, and I'm glad of the calm. It is drizzling now, but going for the mail will not be the precarious run it was yesterday. I was afraid of skidding off the causeway into the water, the tide the highest I have seen there. It's rather exciting and I came home with a huge pouchful of mail like a hunter with a "good bag." Amongst others there was a letter from Bill Brown who, like me, is emerging from depression into a good time of work again. As always his letter made me happy and made me think. Why is it that the contemplation of a painter and his struggles seems more acceptable than that of a writer with his endless words to set down? The sketches that we see later on paper are visible, the problem as it is solved is visible; whereas most of the writer's "sketches" are in his mind, like terrible knots to be unravelled, and the concentration required is of a different order, partly because there is so little "métier," such as brushes to be washed, a canvas to be stretched, and actual semi-mechanical tasks such as filling in a background. I was so moved by Bill's quote (I think he got it from Tillie Olsen) about Cézanne by Rilke,

As regards work, he says that up to his 40th year he had lived as a Bohemian. Only then, in his friendship with Pizzaro, did work dawn on him—to such an extent that he did nothing but work for the last 30 years without real pleasure it seems, in continual rage, ever at odds with his every endeavor, none of which appeared to him to achieve what he regarded as the ultimate desirable . . .

Old, ill, worried every evening to the point of unconsciousness by the regularity of his daily work (so much so that he often went to bed at six o'clock as soon as it became dark after a supper mindlessly eaten) surly, mistrustful, he hoped from day to day still to attain that triumph . . . and does not know whether he has really succeeded. And sits in the garden like an old dog, the dog of this work which calls him again and again and beats him and lets him go hungry. And still he clings with all his strength to this incomprehensible 'master'.

It is true for me that the writing of a novel is that sort of tussle, and that it gives me very little pleasure while I am doing it because the effort is so great. Not so with poems that pounce out of nowhere. The writing of a poem even when it goes through many drafts and even revising a poem cold as I am doing now with the new book, is a kind of intense trance of joy. There is no comparison.

But I find the journal suspect because it is almost too easy. It is a low form of creation.

Saturday, January 27th

WHEN I GET INTERRUPTED as I did twice in the middle of the morning by telephone calls yesterday, I feel as frustrated as a spider whose web is torn across by a passing dog. Once the continuity is broken it may take the whole next hour to get back to where I was, and then it is time to walk Tamas, and the work day has been literally "wasted."

The endless rain and drizzle is getting to be boring and depleting. This afternoon I am going to take a holiday from letter writing and try the new washer-dryer that has just been installed next to the guest bathroom. It has taken me six years here to get up my courage to spend all that money for such a mundane thing, but I think the decision had to do with a far more important one, the decision to stay here until I die or cannot manage the stairs, and so give up all ideas of some other solution which might have provided companionship. Maybe this is the year for tearing hopes up like pieces of paper and making a new start. I have got to bear the loneliness for the sake of the kind of uninterrupted routine I have here in the winter, when the day has a slow rhythm, and my mind is most alive. Granted that without personal relations to chew on, without some nourishment from outside besides books, my mind would not be alive and I would become as sluggish as a barge moored on a canal! But what I have here is a permanent haven for work, and work matters most.

I hope I can stick to my plan not to do any poetry readings for a year starting in June. Even now I begin to be anxious about the stiff lecture schedule in March that takes me to Wabash and Olivet and then to San Francisco for a tough week, four poetry readings in a row. That is more than I have done before, but the thought that the Library of Congress in late April will be the last public appearance for a year makes it all seem more possible, a last ordeal and then peace of mind for a time.

And now I'll see if I can remake the torn web after yesterday's interruptions.

Wednesday, January 31st

IT IS REALLY a lugubrious piece of extended bad weather we are suffering—no sun, day after day of drizzle with periods of heavy rain, one after another. Yesterday there were some strips of crimson through the gray mass as the sun rose, and I managed to walk the animals between showers. But at least it looks as though I would get to Andover on Thursday for a poetry reading there without anxiety about hazardous driving. I don't really mind the gray weather because I'm working well, and so much is going on inside me these days.

I have been in Paradise all month reading Virginia Woolf's fourth volume of letters and the biography of E. M. Forster, grazing with immense pleasure in those rich pastures. We all have our ideas of Heaven. S. S. Koteliansky's was an island where he, D. H. Lawrence, Katharine Mansfield, and Aldous Huxley would all live together and write in peace. For some people the eighteenth century, when an enlightened person could encompass more or less all that was known in the arts and sciences, has seemed an ideal world, in contrast to the end of the twentieth century when most of us haven't the foggiest idea about how man got to the moon, or for that matter how hundreds of appliances we use every day work—television remains a total mystery to me, for example—a century in which we are bombarded by needs all over the world and political crises which we are helpless to solve, when the post does not bring a letter from Madame de Sévigné, but tons of waste matter, demands for help, and advertisements—a wasteful clamor we have to try to shut out.

My heaven is Bloomsbury, as Virginia Woolf so perfectly described it in a letter to her nephew, "We are merely wild, odd, innocent, artless, eccentric and industrious beyond words." The richness and variety of what they produced is simply astounding, from Woolf's and Forster's novels to Keynes' economic theories and Leonard's, to the paintings of Vanessa Bell and Duncan Grant,

to Roger Fry's art criticism, to Strachey's style as a histo-
rian. They were incredibly productive, but the main
charm is not that, but is, I think, the honesty, courage, and
taste with which they honored and explored personal relationships. That is why it looks like heaven from here in
York where there is no one with whom I can share perceptions, passions, questions, fears and doubts as they did
with each other over a long period of years. They were
unshockable except by vulgarity or coarseness of sensibility, and they were idealists. They fought for what they
believed in: Virginia's nephew, Julian Bell, the poet, was
killed in Spain, and in World War I his elders fought jing-
oism and were, most of them, pacifists which took more
courage perhaps even than it did here during the Viet-
nam war. Virginia Woolf was an articulate feminist—we
are only beginning to acknowledge the worth of *Three
Guineas* where she used humor to devastating effect on
the pomposity of the bemedalled, bewigged, and gener-
ally grotesque costumes in which men asserted their
power and their glory.

   They had such a vivid sense of life that I have been
haunted for forty years or more by that laughter of Virginia Woolf's, as I heard it when I went to Tavistock
Square for tea, like some saving grace never to be found
again. Why was the conversation so good? Partly because
everything including private life could be openly discussed (Virginia Woolf loved to pin one down to what was
really happening in one's life), and partly because the
frame of reference was so wide. I got a little taste of it long
ago, and it has set a standard that I have never met since.
The sheer energy required to work as hard as they did and
still be as social as they were is rare. I could never myself
sustain the pace that V. Woolf did. Astonishing fertility.

Monday, February 5th

AND AT LAST real winter weather with sunlight, snow on the ground, crisp air. After all those dark days last week it is exhilarating.

Sometimes so much happens in a few days that it is hard to get it all sorted out. On Thursday I went down to Phillips Academy at Andover for two nights to talk to faculty and students and read poems as the Stearns Memorial lecturer. I set out in a happy frame of mind, looking forward to delicious meals at the Inn: a kind of holiday. This time the poems I had chosen to read were built around the theme, "The Joys and Hazards of Being a Poet," how to keep oneself open and vulnerable and still keep one's balance. That is it in a nutshell. It is not easy. Six of the good poets of roughly my generation have been suicides. If I have survived it may be because I can write novels, journals, and so on in the dry spells. I have the tools for climbing out of depression as I am doing now.

It all began well with cocktails with the English faculty and dinner at the Inn, followed by an informal talk about teaching poetry around Kelly Wise's fireplace. But after midnight I woke in a cold sweat and felt so ill and so strange that I thought for an hour that it must be a heart attack and for about fifteen minutes I believed I was dying. My hair was plastered to my head, my pajamas soaked. My teeth were chattering though the room had been uncomfortably hot. Finally I threw up repeatedly for an hour and got some relief. At three that morning it seemed impossible to read poems at ten to the students and give a big speech at eight that night. But by morning I was able to swallow some tea and slept till nine again and finally dressed and went downstairs. I found that I could manage, read animal poems to a kind and attentive group of students, and realized that I was going to make it. I slept for the rest of the day, and the speech went well that evening. Oh the relief of that! Of having a voice and finding the energy to project to a full house, after all, the guardian angel not far off. For how could I have done it without her help?

Next day I signed books at the Andover Bookstore, under perfect circumstances, for I sat at a round table by an open fire with chairs placed around it so people could sit down while they waited. A fine crowd showed up including a small child, a girl about eight who solemnly handed me a poem she had spoken and her mother written down for her. It was a good poem about the sun. A grandmother came with her little granddaughter bearing two red and white tulips for me. I had an argument with a woman who insists she must use a pseudonym. A former classmate of mine at the High and Latin School in Cambridge showed up, and several friends of friends. What is difficult on these occasions is to get the names one is to inscribe rightly spelled and at the same time pay attention to the *person*. Each has something he or she wants to tell me about himself or herself, about what some book or poem of mine has meant, so one has, in about sixty seconds, to recognize, to acknowledge, to respond on several levels at once. I was tired at the end of an hour and a half, but it was well worth the effort.

How happy I was to get home, unpack, read the mail, and then lie down with Tamas and Bramble and be very still for an hour, slowly "coming back" into myself.

Wednesday, February 7th

EXTREME COLD for days now with wind chill way below zero but I love the cold and the bright snow and so do the animals. Last night there was a ring around the moon and this morning I was woken at six by a blood-red sky, so nature as well as Don Kent is predicting snow.

I came upon a paragraph in the Forster biography last night that so exactly expresses my own logos at the moment, I must copy it out. It is from a letter by Forster to a friend (September 15, 1924):

I have wondered—not whether I was getting down or up, which is too difficult, but whether I had moved at all since King's. King's stands for personal relationships, and these still seem to me the most real things on the surface of the earth, but I have acquired a feeling that people must go away from each other (spiritually) every now and then and improve themselves if the relationship is to develop or even endure. *A Passage to India* describes such a going away—preparatory to the next advance, which I am not capable of describing. It seems to me that individuals progress alternately by loneliness and intimacy, and that legend of the multiplied Krishna serves as a symbol of a state where the two might be combined. The 'King's' view oversimplified people: that I think was its defect. We are more complicated, also richer, than it knew, and affection grows more difficult than it used to be, and also more glorious.

January was rich in that kind of loneliness and I worked well, and even began to catch up on letters. Now

life is silting up again and I feel agitated like a compass
gyrating around before it settles at a fixed point. Today I
have to go to Westbrook near Portland to meet with the
juries of Spectra I, which is to be a festival of Maine
women artists in May (I helped judge the poets). There is
an interview on Saturday and letters have piled up again
because I was away for two days last week. The income
tax has to be faced, a complicated hassle.

But the days lighten and yesterday there were titmice
and purple finches at the feeder. What a joy!

Friday, February 9th

LAST NIGHT I went out for supper, something I rarely do.
A brilliant starry sky and the snow lighting up the borders
of the road in a rather spooky way. I went for the first time
to Bob and Donna Johnston's house and what pleasure it
was to walk into a house so full of life! The first thing I saw
was an aquarium with five turtles sleeping there on sand.
One is fifteen years old, Bob told me. Four Siamese cats
sat here or there on high stools or anywhere high up in the
kitchen, looking like blue-eyed owls. And there were
hanging plants everywhere. Out in a small goose-house I
could not see among the pines on their hillside they have
geese!

Bob is public relations director at the Portsmouth ship-
yard and Donna teaches fifth grade. They are readers.
Our talk ranged from Philip Booth's poems to politics to

cooking—Donna is a great cook and the enormous kitchen and dining room is where we sat beside an old wood-burning stove. When I left, Donna gave me what she called "a CARE package" containing Valentine cookies with pink icing, a jar of the Coquilles St. Jacques mixture we had had for supper, a large piece of heavenly gingerbread which we had had as dessert, and a jar of homemade raspberry jam plus onion bread she had also made. Opening that paper bag when I got back was rather like reading a poem, so full of imagination and kindness it was, a poem by Marianne Moore. It had been a happy evening. But I am paying for it this morning with a slow start. Any digression now holds up the novella.

This is not a very good time for me because I'm trying to do too many things. Letters have piled up, the income tax takes hours of petty figuring and sorting out of checks and so on, and the journal as well as the novella are always there, waiting to pounce. How to handle it all? Yesterday I decided to try alternate days, write letters one afternoon and do the income tax the next day, and perhaps the journal too only every other day. It does not help that men are here putting vinyl siding on the house and the hammering in irregular eruptions all morning long sometimes gets on my nerves, not when I am working well, but when I am twiddling my thumbs trying to concentrate. The effort of writing itself is nothing. It is that intense concentration, the imaginative heave before I can write a word that is exhausting. I am an hour late this morning, so I must get into racing trim at once. "Ready, on your mark, get set, go!"

Tuesday, February 13th

WHERE HAVE FOUR DAYS GONE? I am suddenly desperate for time, while energy flows out in the bitter cold. It has been ten below zero every day for a week, and little by little I feel myself leaning toward sleep like an animal that longs to curl up somewhere and hibernate. Yet the light is dazzling, even at night when the full moon reflected on snow makes the darkness gleam.

On Saturday Constance Hunting came to interview me for her little magazine, the *Puckerbrush Review.* She founded it in order to be able to review books of poems and other books that rarely get a break anywhere else. It is a distinguished production that sets a high standard and I'm happy that she will do a piece on me to accompany an interview and review of *A Reckoning* by Karla Hammond. We had a splendid talk by the fire in the library, then oyster stew for lunch; yet this pleasure took the day and I have been catching up ever since.

One reason I love living in Maine is that so many spontaneous efforts to help the arts spring up here. There is little or no money, but people care, and somehow or other things are accomplished. Maine is still a state of small operations based on individual initiative. That is precious.

Sunday I woke with a streaming nose and was "under the weather" as my mother used to say. I had invited Susan Garrett to help me eat a really good beef stew I

made the other day. We see each other rarely but she and
George are among my few "root friends" in York. He is
away teaching at the University of Michigan this term,
and Susan is in her second year as administrator of the
York hospital, the center of that whirlpool of doctors,
nurses, patients, the one who acts as a buffer for all com-
plaints . . . what exhausting days! When I consider a life
like hers, so *given* and driven and how she is, nevertheless, an ever-flowering, responsive, caring person, I feel a
kind of awe. Who has managed to write of women's lives
well enough?

An Episcopal minister has discovered me and in a
second letter, after one full of praise, berates me for the
lack of strong men in my novels. It is a fair criticism,
especially as he starts out by admitting that women are
stronger than men (I hate generalities though). I suppose
the lack of strong men is because I am more aware, being
a woman myself, of what burdens women take on than I
am of those men take on. And also that women in literature written by men are so rarely great *persons*. Henry
James comes to mind as an exception to this generality.

Saturday, February 17th

SOMETIMES the hour I spend in bed from six to seven
having my breakfast and thinking leads to a door opening
and then the day starts well. Today that was so. I have
been so overwhelmed by the piles of letters at my desk
and the daily struggle lately, three hours in the afternoon

trying to catch up, that I had a bad attack of diverticulitis
and spent all day Thursday lying around. The pain was
bad, but mostly I felt incapable of the smallest effort, and
slept until ten in the morning and again all afternoon.

Yesterday I felt much better, but the cesspool froze
(and no wonder after ten days of this relentless below zero
weather) and that meant agitation and waiting for the
men to come, delightful humorous young men who
worked hard and fast and got everything cleared out and
functioning in two hours. I did no real work, only a few
letters. This morning I realized with astonishment that,
after all, the letters were written to thank me for the
public letters that are my poems and novels and memoirs,
to thank me for bringing something alive in the writer, so
why do I have to answer? Someone gives one a present
and is thanked and usually one doesn't answer the thanks!
But how not to answer, for instance, a letter that came
yesterday from a ninety-five-year-old who, as she said, "in
a moment near self-pity" was delighted by my poem
about the jay and told me that just as she was reading it
again, a jay came to her feeder. How not clasp that out-
stretched hand from ninety-five to sixty-six? Still, I am
trying, out of desperation, to use the form letter I had
printed more than a year ago, explaining my plight, and
yesterday I addressed two of these. Doing it leaves me
feeling empty and sad.

Yesterday came from England Mary Stella Edward's
Before and After, a volume of poems in memory of her
lifetime friendship with Judith Ackland, the artist, who
died in 1971. This morning in bed I read them through and
felt the good tears flowing down my cheeks for the first
time since Christmas. These poems celebrate a long devo-
tion and sharing between two remarkable women, one a
poet, the other an artist (though Mary Stella is also a fine

painter of water colors)—and what the poems did was to open my grief about Judy and give it a blessing. This is what poetry can do, to make the unbearable bearable and to release grief. Here is one called,

Thomas Hardy Perhaps

Who would one more expect to see
Standing beside the leaning stone—
Such worn names long include his own—
Than he who would have noticed such things
As the fresh-cut flowers and the instant bee
Visiting them as though they grew,
And the feather from some bird now flown
That left a message as it flew
To link the present and the gone.

Morgan Mead comes for the night tonight. I look forward very much to a good long talk with "one of my people," for that he surely is. It means exchanging the very marrow of our lives, and feeling the support of understanding. Yet there must be nearly forty years between us, nothing at all, when it comes to essences.

Monday, February 19th

MORGAN arrived rosy and shining with a knapsack of things to tell me and bearing a superb bottle of wine to have with our roast lamb. At his age so much happens in a few months, and even at my age in a life like mine, that we had a great deal to exchange, plunging in at once, while I was making tea and lighting the fire.

I feel sure that he is a writer, as sure as one can be about anyone, but it is always hard to convince one's family (he is the eldest of six children, expected to "do well" in some professional field, of course) that such a precarious adventure is not mere self-indulgence. He has been a teacher, and a good one, in fifth and sixth grade, and now he is taking the risk of being a writer. What he needs is a success, a story sold to the *New Yorker* (he has sold one to *Yankee* sometime ago), or the *Atlantic* and both have shown interest, but so far no luck.

I believe Morgan is a novelist, partly because his passion is family life and he needs space for the quality of life he describes. While we talked I remembered that for a year I had written short stories after my theatre company collapsed. Previously I had written only poems. None of these stories sold but an editor at Houghton Mifflin told me, after reading them, that he felt I was a novelist and should try a novel. It seemed next to impossible, but I thought about it and roughed out the first part of *The Single Hound*. Houghton Mifflin gave me a contract and $250 advance on the strength of a hundred pages, and that paid my passage to England. My father was still giving me $100 a month allowance, and that gave me the magical spring when I first met the Huxleys, Koteliansky, James Stephens. On such slim threads of chance are our lives suspended!

Why do I think Morgan is a writer? Perhaps because he is an extraordinarily sensitive register of feeling, his own and other people's. He is a born friend for both men and women, and also children for whom he has a special regard. He observes. He listens. He is what Henry James says the writer must be, "one on whom nothing is lost." And in a quiet way, without arrogance, he is tough about doing what he wants to do and not being deflected. But that doesn't mean he will not suffer agonies of self-doubt and bitter disappointments along the way.

For me he is a joy, a rare friend, with whom I exchange everything that is happening to me. There are not so many of those these days. So, though I may have suggested above that our relationship is that of an "arrived writer" (more or less arrived!) with a beginner, that would not be an accurate assessment. Quite simply I can be wholly myself with him and know that I am in the deepest sense understood.

Tuesday, February 20th

I GOT BACK to the novella yesterday, a leap into the dark. And now it is about half written I wonder whether I can ever pull anything worth publishing out of it. There are so many things I had in mind to say here that aren't getting in . . . about money, for instance, the kinds of things the rich take for granted, and the kind of power they exercise without even being aware of it.

I stayed up again to see the second part of *Roots*. This is the new *Roots*, taking the black family on into the nineteenth century when it starts. The danger, not averted here, is the danger of stereotypes—*all* the whites are corrupt! That is going a bit too far. Yet the immense power whites had over blacks did corrupt. One sees the lasting effects every day, the Southerners who feel they "understand" the blacks because they have always had black servants who still say "Yassum." The most powerful moment last night was when the upright black father of the clan involved runs into the white colonel who has betrayed his formerly liberal position because he can't get elected if known as a "nigger lover." The colonel does have a conscience and is eaten up by it, and as he rides by the black man he stops to say "You and I understand each other. I've always known what you were thinking and you've always known what I was thinking." The black man (this episode comes shortly after a lynching) doesn't smile or bow, but looks the colonel straight in the eye and says "No, I've always known what you were thinking but you have never known what I was thinking." Forever and ever the blacks had to play a role, the role of subservience, had to accept constant humiliation in order to survive. The price of the vaunted warmth between the races in the South, "we understand them," was achieved at a very high price, the corruption of a whole race, or rather of both races.

It is when I think about this that I have to bow my head before the shining courage of Martin Luther King. We all in the USA carry such wounds deep down inside us, such terrible wounds.

In a strange way I am saying something about this in my novella. Wherever one human being humiliates another both are corrupted.

Friday, February 23rd

IT ALL COMES BACK to consciousness. When we feel superior to anyone over a length of time, when above all, we have superior *power,* the sneer even when clothed in humor ceases to be conscious. Little by little we take it for granted that those in our power must be inferior. When this goes on for generations it is extremely damaging. And when bigotry is attacked from within, the result is outrage . . . as we see in Boston where the Irish react with fury to laws that impose desegregation and busing. At least in the South there was some sense of *noblesse oblige.*

It is suddenly very warm . . . unbelievable to hear gentle rain against the windows last night! But the immediate effect on me anyway is exhaustion, like a woman who has held herself taut against high wind and falls down when she can relax again. I'm in misery about the novella, stuck, and (much worse) a little bored. So I'm giving myself a holiday tomorrow to go and see Woodson and Barton in North Parsonsfield. We haven't met since just before Christmas and their winter, unlike ours, has been full of deep snows as well as cold.

Saturday, February 24th

THERE IS SOMETHING soothing about a rainy day. It inspires me to sudden domestic fury and I have just washed some blouses and cleaned the small oven which made me wince every time I opened the door. In a way my idea of a holiday is to be able to do such things in peace, no compulsion even to walk Tamas. The animals take to their beds and sleep for hours.

Yesterday was pure heaven . . . a milky gentle day, with soft blue skies appearing now and then and sunlight for a few moments touching the white clapboard of an old farm as I drove over to North Parsonsfield. As soon as I got past Alfred the farms were half buried in snow. I couldn't see the White Mountains when I got to the high hill where there is a great view because of the haze, but it was a beautiful drive anyway, and at last I saw the dark red barn of Deer Run Farm behind five-foot walls of snow on either side of the road.

I was early and sat in the car for a moment drinking it all in, a Muscovy duck coming out of the barn, the great door open and the back door open too, so I could see right through, bird feeders everywhere with siskins, nuthatches, and chickadees weaving their swift patterns in the air. And then Ann and Barbara saw me and we had to hug each other hard as it is such a long time since I have been able to come to the farm.

Of course I had first to go into the barn and see the

multitude of hens in their various shelters. Amazing that they survived the terrible cold all these months, all except some old Bantams that Ann finally took into the house cellar during this bitter cold week. She sells eight dozen eggs a week, not bad for winter yield. We came in through the shed where Barbara is working at a big sculpture of a doe with fawns and has just finished a miniature soapstone round of a mouse with two infants at her teats; the shed has that peculiar smell of chipped rock, a clean slightly acrid smell. From there, still not inside the house, we came to Ann's plants under lights—how green and healthy they all are!—big pots of parsley, begonias, several different ferns, and a huge shiny-leaved Streptocarpus that she gave me for the plant window here. Finally we came into the kitchen where the small potbellied wood stove gave a warm welcome, as in spite of the warm weather, I felt the snow and damp in my bones. Immediately Edward, their pet robin, saved four years ago as a baby, flew over my head. He is a very present presence and sings a lot, a new phase.

When I went to the bathroom there were the doves in their cage. Ann told me she had let them out to fly around the house the other day and they reacted well to sudden freedom. Edward often stays near them and perches on the cage. The pet squirrel, Jonathan, in Ann's studio is flourishing—such a huge tail and such a delightful silvery tummy! The house is tiny and full of life; animals, birds, and plants everywhere, hanging in the windows and filling the small porch where we ate our lunch. There we sat and watched outdoor birds flying about and standing on the snow up to the sills so they seemed to be in the room at times. It is a rich kingdom, the kingdom of a heaven created with love and very hard work by two remarkable women.

I always have to see everything first, and then finally we sit down for a long catching up with our lives and all that has happened in the last months. While we were having our drinks a neighbor dropped by and I was happy to meet one of their friends from the village. They have only been in North Parsonsfield for two years, but already, as I found in Nelson twenty years ago, there is a nucleus of neighbors. Ann's herbs for sale and the plants, as well as the eggs, have brought people in who might have been too shy otherwise. Besides, the quality of life at Deer Run Farm must attract in itself, as well as astonishing some of the natives. They must have gone by in their pickups and been amused to see two middle-aged women up on ladders painting the house and huge barn themselves. And they were undoubtedly aware of a garden being created and of wood being chopped and hauled, and of a snowblower being worked mighty hard this winter.

Heaven has to be earned!

Later

When I called Ann to thank her and B. she told me that Jonathan sleeps in a large pickle jar with some scraps of soft cloth in it. These he takes out and airs every day and then remakes a nest. I wish I could see this. The jar-nest is buried under shavings, so I didn't even know it was there.

Monday, February 26th

I HAVE BEEN SITTING for minutes watching the waves break over the end of the field. It is exciting when this happens because it means a big storm. This is a real Nor'-easter, blowing a mixture of sleet, rain, and snow that is going to make for a precarious sortie to get the mail this morning. There is a total eclipse of the sun which we won't see of course, but that means a very high tide, two or three feet higher than normal at ten this morning. From my window here in my study I get a wide expanse of ocean, and, as I can't see the rocks below the field, it looks now as though the waves were running right over it, spreading their foam on the snow.

Yesterday was a happy day, soft, misty, springlike, and I went over to Heidi and Harry Lapirow's for Sunday dinner: such a feast of lobster in a cream sauce, with a heavenly dessert, strawberry mousse molded into lady fingers. A Sunday dinner *en famille* is a great joy and takes me back to my childhood, and with the dear Lapirows I feel like a child of the house. Their Himalayan cat, Mani, has become a raving beauty with a huge fluffy tail and those amazing blue eyes. She likes to pat people's hair and climbed up on my shoulder to play with mine and gently bite as well.

The day was happy, too, because after four months, the *New York Times* printed a long splendid letter from the LeShans to defend *A Reckoning* against Dickstein's mean review. I had given up hope that any one of the twenty or more letters I know were sent in, would be published. Dickstein in her answer to this sticks to her guns that it is a concealed homosexual novel.

As I think over all the letters I have had on this book the one that pleased me the most, I think, was from Emery Neff who taught comparative literature at Columbia (he and his wife among my dear Nelson friends). He says

A Reckoning liberates from primal fears: fear of sexual deviation, fear of dying. Laura frees herself from resentment against her mother (conventional sex repression) and from the hospital, a mechanism for unnatural prolongation of life. All in a small space, vividly detailed. *De Nobis Fabula.* You assure us, in our eighties, that we can to a large extent control the circumstances of our dying and forgive wounds received in the course of living.

Dickstein failed to see the wood for the trees. And because of her misuse of a poem to prove her point I cannot but believe that she had made an *a priori* judgment.

Last night reading Virginia Woolf's journal written at the time *Jacob's Room* came out, I noted, "The only review I am anxious about is the one in the *Times Literary Supplement:* not that it will be the most intelligent, but it will be the most read and I can't bear people to see me downed in public." *Exactly.*

Tuesday, February 27th

THE SUN IS OUT after two gloomy days of sleet and rain, dangerous driving, and a hard crust on the snow, so walking Tamas yesterday I didn't enjoy it and was glad to have to take with me a new cane with a pointed tip. In the mail Erica Jong's fourth book of poems, *At the Edge of the Body*. I was a little reluctant to open it for fear I might not like it and I am touched that she sent it, though unsigned, touched because I had refused to blurb her second novel. I knew what I was doing as the publishers sent proof shortly after Erica had called me "a national treasure" and shortly after we had a brief friendly meeting at Nortons' in New York. It must have seemed churlish not to return in kind such kindness, but I could not assent to a Lesbian passage in it, damaging to women, and exactly what men most want to hear. It was a rather excruciating decision and seemed at the time like another piece of the bad luck that attends me wherever any chance of acclaim is in the offing.

The poems are full of life; I see Erica as a kind of Ceres scattering a million seeds in order that one poem may prove alive. It's a profuse rich sensuous talent, nothing narrow or self-conscious about it, one might say a rich *ego*. No one exists outside her self, really, but that self is such a rich self, rich and womanly. There are few poets who can be called womanly. I heartily assent to her words about the hard line women-against-men,

> When Persephone stays in hell
> the entire year,
> then how can spring
> begin?

What she calls "my poetry suit" is a rainbow suit and sometimes delightfully a clown suit, and in her poetry suit she takes big risks and is honest. I like this book a lot. An explosion of seeds and flowers.

My doubts about it are self-doubts. I want something harder of myself, harder in the sense of the critical self working in harness with the explosion of feeling. I would not allow hyperbole, the play of fancy, play with words as she does. I would want to tighten and hammer into shape. But then a line of Frost's leaps to mind, "We love the things we love for what they are." Isn't there room for Erica and May in the same world? Aren't both kinds of poetry valid?

The men who have been hammering vinyl siding on the house for weeks, in all the fierce cold, are finishing up now, right outside the dormer windows of my study. I shall be glad to work without this constant erratic noise. But my fears that the pale yellow would ruin the charm of this formerly chocolate-ice-cream-brown shingled house have proved wrong. It looks airy and charming in its new suit.

Thursday, March 1st

IN THE MAIL yesterday out of the blue came a letter from
my mother written on December 31, 1917. It had been
found by the daughter of the recipient, Mrs. Moore, with
her mother's papers. After I had read it, I felt such a pang,
for what happens to such a letter? And then I realized I
could copy it here and so not lose it. We were living then
in a three-room apartment at 10 Avon Street in Cambridge, and had, of course, had no word from Belgium
from the dear friends there, no word as to whether our
house in Wondelgem had been blown up. 1917 was that
darkest year of the war before the United States came in.
My mother writes,

Dear Mr. and Mrs. Moore,

We all send to you and your children sincere good wishes
for this New Year . . . May sends this card which she coloured
(over a rough sketch of mine) entirely herself to 'Dorothea and
John Moore over in France' with her love. And I have made you
this tiny basket of flowers, thinking all the time of the sweet
dear flowers you sent me this summer . . . I have woven in
among them the special wish that you may have many many of
the precious *little* happinesses of every day—the ones that
come right beside big sorrows, and which I know you all are
lavish to others with—It is a very humble wish compared to
those we only dare form in our hearts this year, but it is because
joy and peace seem so far away that we need so badly the "little
happinesses."

Yours very sincerely,

E. Mabel Sarton

So much of my mother flows out to me from this letter that I sat in the car after reading it there, deeply shaken. She had such a gift for life, for just those small joys of which she speaks. The basket of flowers she embroidered for the Moores will have been in brilliant colors, emerald green, soft oranges, pinks, blues, blacks. Color to her, as it is for me, was a kind of food. And the hardest thing at 10 Avon Street was that she couldn't have a garden there, not even a tiny plot.

But what resilience she had, what power to renew herself over and over again, although, unlike my father who burrowed happily into the Widener Library and rooted himself there, she remained an uprooted and transplanted person to the end.

Friday, March 9th

THE NOVELLA is coming to a climax so for the days before March 5th when I had to go to Worcester to read poems, I worked only at that and let this journal go. One of my reasons for accepting an engagement was to have an excuse to see Sue Hilsinger and Lois Brynes and the old house they bought last fall in Auburn—what a joy it is to see them in their own home, an eighteenth-century house with the unusual charm of having many large rooms, six fireplaces. They have space out of doors also, with four acres of field and woods, two large garden plots, neglected and jungly but there to be rescued. Unfortunately both days were rainy, but I did get out between showers for a little exploring. Since they moved in, in late autumn, the spring is going to be a series of surprises as they learn what plants there are. Lois is a plant enthusiast but has never had the experience of gardening in any big way. Today I am mailing her Burpee's seed catalogue so she can dream up a bed of annuals and have picking flowers this summer. We murmured words like "wheelbarrow" and "pitchfork." They are starting from scratch, the dears, and I tremble before the ordeal ahead and long to be a millionaire and send them hundreds of daffodils to naturalize this autumn.

I loved being there, for these are "my people." We laugh at the same things, have the same anxieties (Sue is a distinguished novelist as well as a professor of literature at Clark University), need to talk for hours, need to have periods of silence. It was an altogether happy time for me, except that I read the novella through and am thoroughly dismayed at how bad it is, flat and (I fear) boring. The problem is partly to find a style for an eighteen-year-old girl who is warm and loving but not in any sense an intellectual . . . What have I got myself in for?

Sue introduced me to a packed house—the reading took place in the public library—and I did well, perhaps because for once the introduction was so perceptive and to the point rather than the usual ramble through "distinctions" culled from *Who's Who*. I love to hear the poems ring out and hear them *land* in that special silence when a large audience is moved. For me a poem is a little like a sheet of music; only when it is "played" can one truly hear it and know what has been set down. Sue said, for instance, that she had never fully understood "The Lady and the Unicorn" until that evening because she had never heard me read it. It is also perhaps that the eye reads too fast, especially the eye of a brilliant and quick intelligence such as hers.

Very rarely do friends of mine, "my people," witness me at work on a public occasion. It was so heartening to hear both Lois and Sue say many times, "I don't see how you do it. . . ." That effort is not the reading itself, which I enjoy in spite of tension and fear beforehand, but is being responsive to so many strangers at the social occasions, in this instance, a dinner beforehand and a reception afterwards.

Yesterday morning I signed books in the Women's Bookstore in Worcester, as I wanted to help Ellen Gardiner who started it a year ago. It is already, I sense, a center for women who need to have a club, a place for "bonding" of their own. And it is good news that there are so many of these centers springing up all over the country. The average person thinks of the women's movement as noisy and radical, perhaps, but here in these small rooms where women can find their own fellowship and communion something is going on of essential value. For a little while the loneliness and sense of isolation can be laid aside. Not a great many people came, but those who did were good to know. All had discovered my work only recently and gone from one book to another, and wanted to tell me what it had meant.

I did feel tired when I got home to the usual avalanche of things that have to be answered, but it was worth it. However, I am increasingly happy to think of a year away from public appearances.

The people I missed because of rain were the dog-people. Sue and Lois have two red Irish setters, and because of the mud in their outdoor enclosure they had to be kept in their own quarters in the house, and I hardly saw them.

Sunday, March 11th

RAIN, RAIN, and more rain. It is dismal. But there are small signs of spring at last. Among the dull brown detritus on the floor of the woods the moss is suddenly emerald green in small cushions, not only emerald but other darker brilliant greens. There are pussy willows beginning to show silvery buds along the stems. I keep forgetting to take my clippers with me on the walk. High boots are needed because of the mud and pools of water in the ruts in the road—mud season, the dankest most colorless time of the year's cycle here.

Snow drops are out around the big maple and crocus are beginning to show hopeful pointed buds here and there.

On Friday the *Paris Review* interviewer was here all day, a young woman just graduated from Radcliffe. I suspect it is her enthusiasm for *Mrs. Stevens* that persuaded the editors to do an interview at last. Of course it took place years ago in my imagination in Part II of *Mrs. Stevens Hears the Mermaids Singing* so there was a curious *déja vu* quality about it for each of us. Without Wanda's enthusiasm no one would have come, but I did feel a little sad that the long-awaited interviewer was not ideal. She did not know the work intimately, and is not a poetry reader. That made me take the bit between my teeth and talk quite a lot about the poems. What was disappointing was the lack of acute questions, the kind of question that can be revelatory for the interviewee. I made an effort to be receptive to what she had to give and to be as helpful as I could, and it may be that it will turn out better than I feared.

There was a good augury as I drove her out to her bus . . . along the dirt road just outside the gates here, I saw the unmistakable large rounded shape of an owl sitting on the telephone wires where a row of wood pigeons often gathers. It is rare to see an owl in broad daylight, so of course I stopped the car. We got out, saw it, a blurred round for a second, and then it rose and flew off on immense silent wings . . . wonderful that unexpected spread, the size of it, and the silence!

I feel better about the novella. In a curious way realizing that something one has made is inadequate provides excitement. I think all the time about what I can do to salvage it. It is poor work because I have failed often to concentrate on detail, to bring a scene alive in concrete terms. Transitions are weak. And the fact that the protagonist is a non-intellectual, rather simple young girl has allowed me to get away with a lax style that simply has to be sharpened and tightened. It is written in the first person. Simply copying the whole thing on the typewriter and revising as I go along will help. But first it has to be completed and I'm awfully afraid I can't manage it before I leave on the lecture trip.

For Olivet, where I go at the end of the month to read poems and appear as judge of their yearly poetry contest, I am judging forty or fifty poems. None are bad, but how I miss form and music! How stale and flat much free verse is! It is not enough to describe accurately and leave it at that. So few of these poets do more than one thing at the same time. Something is described but nothing else is evoked by the description.

Monday, March 12th

FOR THE FIRST TIME in seven days a round red sun burst
up from the horizon this morning and we are to have a
cold bright day for a change. It is I who am dull and dreary
this morning, half awake and unable for the moment to
imagine getting to work on the novella.

Last night I went on a real jag reading the Flannery
O'Connor letters and maybe that is why I am tired this
morning. They are a major experience for me. It is interesting that Catholic writers—I think of Mauriac as well as
O'Connor, and even Dante—find it so much easier to
write of hell than of heaven. But I'm in no state to pursue
this.

I went over to Heidi's for Sunday dinner yesterday and
much enjoyed seeing her with her eleven-year-old grandson, Chipper, whom she is taking to North Conway for a
week's skiing this morning. Imagine having a grandmother who skis down mountains and is also the captain
of her own sailboat and a licensed navigator! Heidi has so
much pluck.

Saturday, March 17th

THE HIATUS has been because I was driving hard to finish the novella. I did so on Thursday and took it in to be xeroxed, so as to have two extra copies to fiddle with. As usual when a work is completed, even only in rough, I feel emptied out, as deflated as a balloon, full of doubts and misgivings. So many people write me that the journals and memoirs and the poems are the better part of my work. And I always remember Virginia Woolf teasing me (when I first met her I had published only one book—of poems) about how much easier poetry is than the writing of novels. I suspect the journal as a form because it is too easy, too quick perhaps. But I still believe that a few of my novels will prove to have value in the end, *Mrs. Stevens, Faithful Are The Wounds, As We Are Now,* and possibly *A Reckoning,* when it comes to be read in depth, and what I actually *said* becomes clear.

The two sins I am accused of in the novels are 1) careless style and 2) over-idealism. "Marriages are not like that." "People do not talk as your characters do," etc. Sometimes letters come as saviors. In the midst of this low feeling about the novels a letter came from my Episcopal minister friend in Chapel Hill saying "You have been a superb writer for a long time, haven't you? I suppose I am first of all conscious of your style—because I am sensitive to this trait, perhaps too much so. But there it is, and I am filled with joy when a writer's style is excellent."

I have worked toward a transparent style, as simple and plain as possible, a tool with which to communicate complex relationships. When I began to write I was praised for a "poetic style," but it is just that I have tried to get rid of as too self-conscious. I have come to believe that too elaborate a style gets in the way, dazzles, but makes a wall between writer and reader. I try for a flowing line that suits breath and the voice, that does not stumble, and people discover this when they read a prose work aloud. (Carol Heilbrun says she did so when she read part of *I Knew a Phoenix* aloud to a class one day.)

The other question is more complex—or maybe simpler, who knows?—and has to do with a vision of life. But I might add that all dialogue in fiction has to be stylized to some extent to give an illusion of reality. No one has ever talked like a Hemingway character though after he had created the pared down speech he uses, life sometimes imitated art. Real people talking are apt to be verbose and repetitive. Virginia Woolf uses to great effect sentences that float off into silence, half-finished. But actual living people rarely do this either. And as for Ivy Compton·Burnett, what actual person ever dealt such blows with such wit and complete command? But in all cases of real art, the writer does have a recognizable voice. I believe that I do.

As for idealism, who is not flawed and human and complex? There are certainly no saints. If the vision of life communicated were unreal why does it speak to so many people of all ages, both sexes and all backgrounds? This is why the letters, whatever burden they present, are really what keep me from despair. Here is one sentence—what a marvelous letter it is that makes its point in a single sentence!—this from a director of nursing in a Vancouver hospital: "The human and artistic integrity of *A Reckon-*

ing is a reprieve. I am afraid we were almost Kübler-Ross'd to death. Thank you."

In the same mail, a letter from a young man in St. Louis who has been having a hard passage in his personal life and writes to me now and then, "Anyway your books are with me. When I was little I carried a bag of animals, plastic small pigs, cows, horses, chickens, my own miniature barnyard, everywhere. Now at twenty-nine, I carry your poems."

Yesterday I took the day off and took the making of an oyster stew to Eleanor Blair. She has graduated from her walker to a four-pronged cane that makes her far more mobile with less effort. She told me triumphantly that she has even climbed the stairs. What joy it was to be in her dear house, so full of life, geraniums in flower in a small window greenhouse, books everywhere, light and peace. At eighty-five she is a marvelous "role model" as today's fashion has the phrase, and I hated to cut the visit short but I wanted to stop and see Judy. Since the disaster of Christmas I have not seen her.

I think she recognized me but I am not sure. Two nurses were making her bed and laughed with real merriment when they forgot, because we were talking, to put in the rubber sheet and had to begin again. Their presence was a help as Judy was totally unresponsive, except that she noticed my green jacket when I took off my coat. I stayed only a quarter of an hour. When I left I turned back at the door and saw her sitting in the only chair in her room, her face still so distinguished, but now a blank mask. She is not lonely, but the isolation of her state struck me like a blow to the heart. To be so helpless to help, and to leave her there lost. She did not look up even as I said goodbye.

Tuesday, March 20th

THE AIR is a little warmer and the sun is out, but it's still a static landscape here, and real spring, a bud swelling on a branch, is a long way off.

I look forward to going to bed these days and reading the Flannery O'Connor letters and shall miss her when the book is finished. Last night I was especially struck by this passage:

> The harshness with which you speak of C. is not justified. She may be basically irreligious but we are not judged by what we are basically. We are judged by how hard we use what we have been given. Success means nothing to the Lord, nor gracefulness. She tries and tries violently and has a great deal to struggle against and to overcome. The violent bear it away. She is much to be admired for not repeating. It is better to be young in your failures than old in your successes.

Something came into my hands by chance that has made me think again about *A Reckoning*. What the fear of communism did to destroy lives and to confuse the minds of the innocent to an unbelievable extent under Senator McCarthy's evil influence, the fear of homosexuality appears to be doing now. Guilt by association will make a reviewer accuse me of cowardice if all my characters are not Lesbians, apparently. If I choose to suggest that a friendship between women may be powerful enough to last a lifetime with very little actual contact, I am lying because I must have meant something else! It will make a reviewer go outside the text for evidence, in this case dig out a poem written thirty years ago and distort its meaning, to fit her preconceived idea of what I am all about and what my work is all about.

If this is the ethos in which I am to operate from now on there is very little point in writing novels. People accused of communist influence during the McCarthy era lost their power to be useful in liberal causes because they had become suspect, like carriers of tuberculosis or some other infectious disease. I have hoped to provide the bridge between women of all ages and kinds, between mothers and daughters, between sisters, between women as friends; (the friendship between Ellen and Christina in *Kinds of Love* is an example), between the old and the young (Mar and Mrs. Stevens) and I have wished to be thought of in human terms. The vision of life in my work is not limited to one segment of humanity or another and it has little to do with sexual proclivity. It does have to do with love, and love has many forms and is not easy or facile in any of them.

But if this reduction of my novels to one theme is a reviewer's point of view, it is not that of my readers. Five per cent or less of the letters I get are from Lesbians. The greatest number are from married women, most of these women with children. And if I represent anything in the public consciousness it is as a solitary. It is my solitude and what I have said about it that has made the link, and made so many women and men I do not know regard me as a friend in whom they can confide.

Saturday, April 14th

A LONG HIATUS because I have been away for eighteen rich and exhausting days, first at Wabash and Olivet colleges for the first week, then Berkeley and San Francisco. I had hoped to keep a journal on the way but it was impossible because of the quick changes. My writing self was submerged and even writing a short note seemed as difficult as though I had been expected to write in Chinese characters! The only jotting I managed was at Olivet.

March 29th, Olivet

It is proving to be a very great effort this trip, and I am gladder than ever that I have decided to take a year off. Yesterday I started talking at eight a.m. over breakfast with Betty Bosworth who had come up from Florida to hear me the night before. At nine, Mark Moor, a delightful senior, picked me up to drive me three hours to a restaurant where kind Olivet people were to meet us for lunch and take me on. I had corresponded with Marlene Kondelik, the librarian, and Elizabeth Selden, wife of an English professor, came with her. We arrived here at three-thirty—by then I had been conversing non-stop for seven and a half hours! But what pleasure to be welcomed by a room prepared for my arrival with fruit in a basket, carefully chosen books, magazines, even a cake of lovely soap in the bathroom, and best of all four daffodils and some pussy willows in a glass. It was the first moment of let-down since I left home three days ago and I fell into bed as soon as I had unpacked until it was time to go over to dinner at the Thomsons, she a poet and painter, he in the English department. We feasted on lamb and rice preceded by a remarkable fluffy lentil soup, with cut up strawberries, peaches, and pears for dessert—quite a contrast to the dinner at a fraternity house in Wabash! I was back in my room by ten, but I figured out that by then there had been eleven and a half hours of conversation plus a long drive that day, so, I decided that it was not old age after all that made me feel completely done in. Just ordinary human fatigue.

I loved the drive, the tilled fields rich and black under great open skies, the lonely farms, and getting to know Mark, a strong liberal, curious about how people live, knowledgeable, and talkative. From him I learned a lot, including the fact that the quiet fields we passed, not by any means in the richest farmland in Indiana, would soon be worth $2500 an acre. Of course what kills the small farmer is the high cost of machinery. It was good to learn that Wabash has a strong endowment and can offer a very large number of scholarships to boys from the state. Mark's father is a truck driver.

(The above is all I managed to write on the whole trip.)

Now back at my desk in York with a brooding gray ocean before me I can begin to sort things out. The problem when I get back is that there is so much to be done here at once, and no time to think about the immediate past. I long for two or three blank days in which to savor what has happened, and indeed to discover what really did happen, and since this journal concerns the inner world, perhaps I had better start with that. Someone had sent me a book sometime ago that I saved for this trip because I like to have reading matter with me that can be taken in small amounts and meditated on. Henri J.M.M. Nouwen's *The Genesee Diary: Report from a Trappist Monastery* proved to be an ideal companion. Nouwen, at a crisis in his priestly life, overwhelmed by the complexities he deals with, longing for some spiritual centering again, was accepted for a seven-month participation in the life of a Trappist monastery, and it is the story of that time of discipline and grace that he tells. All the way along, however tired I was, this book was there like good bread, and nourished me.

On June 30th he wrote,

This morning, during his weekly conference, John Eudes made a remark about the relationship between solitude and intimacy that touched me deeply. He said, 'without solitude there can be no real people. The more you discover what a person is, and experience what a human relationship requires in order to remain profound, fruitful, and a source of growth and development, the more you discover that you are alone—and that the measure of your solitude is the measure of your capacity for communion. The measure of your awareness of God's transcendent call to each person is the measure of your capacity for intimacy with others. If you do not realize that the persons to whom you are relating are each called to an eternal transcendent relationship that transcends everything else, how can you relate intimately to another at his center from your center?'

Monday, April 16th

IT IS STRANGE how difficult it is to go backward in a journal to the immediate past. I really don't want to talk about my journey, perhaps only suggest a few fruitful images. Twice I had time with Jungian friends whom I had previously known only by letter. At the end of the rainy week at Wabash and Olivet, Bill Buchanan, a professor in the English department, kindly drove me to Apple Farm where I had twenty-four hours of peace and communion with Helen Luke and her two confreres. My room in the guest house had a big window, and there I sat looking down at a small apple tree where a bird feeder hangs; cardinals, juncos, chickadees came and went, and next morning a brilliant cock with two hens ambled past. But the charming thing was to lift my head and see, up the steep hill, as though in the upper corner of an illuminated manuscript, three or four sheep and several lambs in a small enclosure. Every now and then the lambs suddenly leapt about then settled down with their somnolent mothers. I must have sat there for an hour before supper, letting the peace soak in, and after so much talk, the silence.

At six, Bill and I went over to the farm for a drink and supper. It is an international community, the three therapists are English (Helen Luke), German-Jewish, and American. They each have private quarters but share meals, and sometimes travel together. Helen has a little house of her own down the road. People come to Apple

Farm for seminars, for therapy, or simply to enjoy peace and quiet. For me it felt like coming home into an atmosphere of intimacy and wisdom I have not experienced in the same way since 33 Avenue de l'Echevinage in Uccles, Belgium, where Jean Dominique and her two friends lived. They were a poet, a novelist, and a teacher, not professional doctors, but they too made an island and a refuge for their friends.

Although I was tired, it was a joy to read some poems after supper, poems Helen Luke and her friends knew well and have even found useful in their work, among them "My Sisters, O My Sisters." Next morning I went over to the little house and had a good long talk with Helen Luke. At seventy-five she communicates an amazing rich psychic energy and joy. That was what I came away with . . . how rare! . . . a heart full of joy. They want me to come back and read for neighbors and friends, as there is, it appears, quite a community settled here around them, and I hope I can.

In my one free day in San Francisco Sheila Moon, a poet and Jungian therapist, gave me a whole day, and my heart's desire which was to go to Muir Woods, the redwood forest in Marin County. I was hungry for the silence of the huge trees, unlike any other, awesome silence because the trees are alive and have been alive for so long, so it is not like a cathedral built of stones, but has the same effect. People talk in hushed voices, and one hears nothing but the sound of the water, the brook that runs through the valley. We walked slowly and talked or were silent, and again I felt the power of presence of someone who has thought and felt deeply and in a wide range. Sheila is a little older than I. We talked about old age. She feels that the pain is not less, but the joys perhaps are greater. I believe that to be true. The pure joys, the joy of a wild flower or a bird, or simply the silence of trees is there in old age because we are less distracted by personal emotion. Is that it?

The eighteen days were a progress toward spring . . . quite overwhelming to arrive in Berkeley the second week and find behind every wall or gate the cherry trees in flower, and lilac, and camellias! The air was cool and bright, perfect days. And there, too, I was able to have two hours of bliss in the botanical garden with Doris Beatty where we picnicked after walking for an hour in a daze of beauty—trillium and all sorts of wild flowers, even California poppies, on the ground, and as we came to a brook tumbling over rocks in small waterfalls, masses of rhododendron and azaleas planted with great skill, so they seemed always airy, not crowded. That was the first day, and after that I had a rather full schedule.

In Berkeley I was warmly welcomed, a welcome that had its apotheosis the last evening when I read poems in the Pacific Theological Union chapel, sponsored by six women's groups. It was rather a cold wet night and I wondered whether anyone would turn up . . . but people were piling in when Doris dropped me off and by the time I stood at the lectern, there was a huge expectant crowd, people sitting on the floor behind me and in the side chapel, standing in the aisles and even finally sitting in the center aisle. A wonderfully giving and quiet audience. In this past year I have three times had the amazing experience of being lifted up by a huge audience, at Radcliffe College in Cambridge, at the Unitarian church in St. Paul last November, and then in Berkeley. I guess I had better stop complaining about not being recognized!

Tuesday, April 17th

AT LAST a little touch of spring! I have my window open up here in my study and can hear the gentle purr of waves and this afternoon I am going to get out into the garden to fertilize the terrace border, the azaleas and rhododendrons, and the clematis.

There are a few more images of the trip that I must record before coming back to the present. Ted Morrison once remarked that poets have no memory because they live so intensely in the present. It is true this morning that the moment, *now,* is so precious as I watch the thin line of white foam along the distant shore and listen to the waves breaking, that I can hardly bear to return to this page, especially as in a few days that scene will be screened out by the leaves of the great oak.

It was a beautiful end to my stay in the Bay area to be with Bill Brown and Paul Wonner—the exquisite order of their house, all white inside where their collection of Kangra and other Indian paintings shine like jewels, their way of life which suits me so well because of all it contains of work and silence and music. How marvelous to be brought a French breakfast in bed with croissants, strong French coffee, and hot milk, and to hear Bill playing Mozart downstairs! We have known each other for forty years, Bill and I. As artists we are all three close in what we have suffered of non-recognition, all three working against the current, suffering periods of depression, battling it all out inside. It refreshes the mind to be with people with whom one shares matters of taste, where nothing offends the spirit or the eye, but all delights. Such order and grace! As usual we got into fits of laughter about nothing at all, talked about books, music, the ludicrous power of fashion in the arts, and reestablished through all this a sense of ourselves, of identity, of being in harmony together.

Bill and I went to take a look at *The Dinner Party,* Judy Chicago's "happening" on show at the San Francisco Museum of Art. It was a fine dream, to celebrate great women of the past, and great goddesses also, by creating for each a dinner place setting. "The project" as the publicity has it "was conceived by a Jewish feminist with the help of Catholic nuns, the Ecclesiastical Stitchers' Guild, Methodist, Baptist, and Episcopalian china painters, and literally scores of researchers and studio assistants. It is a non-traditional work of art created with very traditional techniques. With deliberate irony Chicago has utilized 'women's techniques' (stitching and china painting) in a 'women's context' (the dinner party) to create a major feminist art statement."

It was moving to think of all these women working together for five years, but when at last Bill and I reached the big room with its triangle of long tables, we suffered shock. The plates are often in high relief, a surrealistic device that also sets into relief the essential vulgarity and cheapness of Chicago's vision. Many appear to be sexual variations on the theme of the vulva. Well, I was sorry not to like it at all, and embarrassed when I was asked a question about it after my reading at the Unitarian church. I told the truth. What else could I do? When something is as highly publicized as this, when everyone feels compelled to admire it, how hard it is to see with a naked eye, to dare see what one has seen! We are led by the media into a false vision and do not even know what has happened to us, how we have allowed ourselves to be betrayed.

Wednesday, April 18th

IN A LETTER from England the other day came a staggering quote by Pirandello: "One cannot choose what he writes—one can only choose to face it." It hit me like a blow because it made me wonder whether I am after all evading a real responsibility, to write, as so many people ask me, a novel about women in love. I feel great resistance to the idea. If I did it, it would not be sexual, any more than my poems are although many have been written for women. The word that comes to mind lately is "bonding" and maybe that is a clue. I am relieved to have set the novella aside. By very hard work I might have salvaged it, but in the end, I think I exorcised something that happened last summer by writing it, and now whatever it has to say seems to me too insignificant to bother with.

I have been hearing from Nancy Ellis, who was a student of mine at Wellesley and is now a doctor working with terminally ill children. The correspondance began about *A Reckoning* but has now begun to come to grips with all kinds of things that concern us both. In her last letter she reaffirmed my own feelings about Ella and Laura. So much pressure is put on me as a coward not to have made them lovers that I read this paragraph in Ellis's letter with relief.

To make Ella and Laura lovers in *A Reckoning* would be to destroy something very special in that book. It may be that sometimes the human connection you describe occurs in some relation to passionate love, but not usually. The connection between Ella and Laura is a fellow-beingness which has been thought to occur only between men, as brothers. *A Reckoning* is important because you show this connection between women in such fashion that it cannot be denied. Perhaps your critic has not recognized that she is seeing something new. Perhaps she is trying to fit Ella and Laura into extant, familiar categories which are inadequate to contain the phenomenon you have written about.

And later on Ellis tells me,

A Reckoning might be myth-making as you conceived it, but it coincides incredibly with the realities I have seen. But one of the difficult things that happens is that the one whom we wish to sit with us cannot be called, or fears to come, because these connections do not follow the rules of the official connection by blood, marriage, legal responsibility, or even passionate love. This generates a very dismal picture of the ability of the living truly to comfort the dying, but this is actually quite consistent with Elizabeth Kübler-Ross's work with dying patients. In my own work, I am trying to develop a sort of insightful imagination, to help patients and their families locate these special connections.

I woke at five and saw a blue sea and a shining sun for the first time in the week I have been home . . . now it is nearly eight and time to take Tamas to the vets for his booster shots. Yesterday the sun went in and clouds covered the sky, but I did manage to get the tradescantia in, and to lime the clematis, so all was not lost.

Saturday, April 21st

A SPARKLING DAY and warmer. Yesterday there was hard frost, a silver field as I looked out at six. Mary-Leigh and Beverly came over from the big house to have supper with me night before last, a yearly Belgian feast we celebrate with asparagus on toast and hard-boiled eggs mashed up, and all covered with melted butter. We had strawberries in whipped cream and kirsch for dessert, and a bottle of Californian Zinfandel I have been saving for an occasion. It was a chance to catch up on all our news while Tamas, and for once, Bramble, went to and fro, asking to be petted. Poor Bramble, chased off by jealous Tamas, walked away, and in true catlike dignity sat in the hall with her back to us—but eventually she relented and returned.

I have been absorbed in a delightful book of Cambridge memories by Marian Cannon Schlesinger. She brings back a whole lost world, it made me dream. This world was fundamentally unmaterialistic—who cared about clothes? About acquiring things? The houses were freezing cold in winter, the food was simple. The luxuries were travel—Marian describes a European trip, nine women, her sisters and mother in a huge open car, driving all over Italy—playing baseball and tennis, having a country place somewhere in New Hampshire or Vermont, rich and passionate conversation at table and continuous involvement in matters of politics, education. No sooner

was a need felt than Marian's mother leapt into action,
bearding the school committee, or writing letters to President Lowell of Harvard.

Thursday, April 26th

A VIOLENT REACTION to all these public appearances was
inevitable, no doubt. But it is becoming clear to me that
just as poems cannot be written on will, so also recovery
from the blows of last November cannot be achieved by
will. The proof is that the "forced" novella has had to be
laid aside, and that I have come inside myself to a dead
end. It is eight a.m., a foggy morning, a few daffodils out
at last. And when I got home yesterday from Washington
I picked a tiny bunch of scillas and glory-of-the-snow,
some small forsythia branches in bud, and a lovely bunch
of daffodils; so the spring I have met this year in three
places away from home is on the way here at last.

How rare it is in the United States to visit a young
family who are putting down roots close to family that has
lived in the same place for three or four generations! I
breathed in the gentle landscape in Lincoln, Virginia
where Henry and Franny Taylor are bringing up their
two small sons on a piece of his father's land and in sight
of the family farm, a brother and sister-in-law across the
valley, and in the small town the old Quaker Meeting
House where the Taylors have worshipped for three generations. The landscape reminds me of a Patinir, the classic pastoral scene, rolling hills, brooks, small woods car-

peted with wild flowers, nothing raw, nothing that hurts
the eye. Henry and I sat on the porch of the house they
partially built themselves and slowly I felt myself landing
after the flight to Dulles and a beautiful drive in evening
light. It was landing in several ways, as Henry and I have
exchanged poems and criticism for seventeen years, but
have rarely had a chance to talk. It was a timeless evening
while Richard, three, and Thomas, eight, had their supper
and the light slowly changed into blue shadow on the hills.
I felt the goodness and liveliness of this marriage during
the whole eighteen or so hours. Henry and Franny work
together and manage to create an atmosphere both orderly and free for the small boys.

The next evening Henry introduced me at the Library
of Congress reading and, much to my astonishment, spoke
as though I had helped him. Of course I am much older
than he, but I had been grateful that a talented young
poet would take time to criticize, and feel that I learned
a lot more from our exchanges than he could have done.
It was a lovely lift into the reading which I had dreaded
(and with reason) because a half hour is a rather awkward
piece of time, not long enough to make a reasonable
whole out of a mere ten or twelve short poems. When
Henry and I walked out onto the stage I was greeted by
a burst of heartwarming and sustained applause, and that
helped too. But I was flustered by the tick of the inner
clock in my head, cut out poems I should have read, and
ended without reading "Gestalt at Sixty" which was the
logical climax on the theme of "becoming." It has always
been my experience that double readings do not work,
especially with a male confrere. Men think nothing of
running over the allotted time. Women are over-con-
scientious.

The best part of the day was earlier, the vision of Washington in its spring dress with all the tulips, dogwood, azaleas out, and the trees in their transparent feathery green before the leaves make them opaque again. The poetry division at the Library gave a luncheon and I had the joy of a half hour alone with Doris Grumbach in the charming drawing room, high up in the Library, looking across at the Capitol.

I have never before been in on the instant success she is experiencing with her novel *Chamber Music.* Some of it was written here, when she spent a month house-sitting two years ago while I was in England. I have known of her anxieties, and the hard job of revising it from third to first person, and now I am witness to its explosively warm reception. The glamor of such an occasion is immense. One feels transported into a salubrious air where huge sums are paid for paperback rights, where all goes well and brilliantly, as deserved. How very rarely that happens! All Doris's friends rejoice, and I felt the glow like a balm. It is good to know that such things can still happen. But I am not surprised that Doris herself begins to be irritated by the time success consumes and to long to get on with her next novel.

How can I help making comparisons? For the moment I have lost faith in my capacity to write. I feel written out, and that there is very little to show for forty years of hard work and hope. I am not eager to get at a new work but terrified of the very idea. I feel boxed in both in my private life and as a poet and novelist. Until last November the phoenix rose again and again from the ashes. Can it be that this time the phoenix died? But I have to believe that I can make a come back eventually. It is too frightening to imagine even for a second that I am finished as a

creator. I have no illusions that it would make much difference, except to me, one way or another, but I cannot
conceive of my life *without* creation. What would become
of me?

Saturday, April 28th

A REALLY TERRIFYING NIGHT of wild rain and wind, doors
banging, and Bramble refusing to come in, so I slept
badly. I had spent the day driving in the rain with the
windshield wipers at top speed to see Laurie whom I have
not seen for ages. Too bad that I could not see out of the
windows as all the familiar landscapes flowed past . . . it
was a little like driving the car under water. My eyes are
tired this morning and I can't shake the depression. Still,
it was lovely to be enfolded once more in Laurie's atmosphere, to be at home and to bask in her gallant spirit, her
tenderness, her eager perceptive talk of books, to rest in
her values which are also mine. We are, each in our own
way, survivors. With her I touch base.

That is what I did also with Margaret Bouton with
whom I stayed in Washington. I have known Miggy since
we first arrived in Cambridge in 1917 and lived across the
street in a three-room apartment opposite the Boutons'
house. We played elaborate games with our dolls (at
Christmas time their front parlor was converted into a
large doll's house.) We cooked tiny meals for our dolls, put
them to bed, dressed them, scolded them, projected on to
them our own desires and needs. In the summer I was

invited to stay with the Boutons at Kearsarge and there
Miggy and I built a small village of twigs and moss in the
woods by a brook. Now Miggy is one of the chief people
in the department of education at the National Gallery
where she works late into the night, and is often recognized on the street by people who have heard her lectures. There is no tension between us. We can take each
other for granted, my "oldest friend" as she says when she
introduces me. Her apartment is high up and peaceful
and there I really rested, and then spent a marvelous
morning the day after my reading, wandering about in
the magical spaces of the new Pei wing of the Gallery. The
past kept coming up . . . a truly marvelous show about
Berenson's methods of attributing paintings, with many
photographs of I Tatti. Miggy and I had lunch in the
charming balcony restaurant and afterwards she took me
around the new office space, not yet inhabited, where she
will shortly move. There, how astonishing, to see a very
tall man with white hair and to realize that this apparition
was Ted Amussen who had been my editor at Rinehart
and Co., my editor at the time of *Faithful Are The
Wounds, The Fur Person,* and three books of poems. And
there we were, each with snow-white hair, hugging each
other.

I feel a little wild and unsettled, longing for time to
remake my nest here, for that is what has to be done.
Yesterday I bought two boxes of pansies in the pouring
rain . . . such a small thing as planting them tomorrow will,
perhaps, do the trick. I feel at present like a baby seal
swimming desperately around in an enormous ocean trying to find some landing. Excruciating loneliness.

Thursday, May 3rd

MY SIXTY-SEVENTH BIRTHDAY. A perfect, still day, sunshine for a change, and an unutterably blue, pale Fra Angelico sea. The daffodils are out in great garlands lighting up the dark brown field, and inside the fence there is a border of hyacinths, scillas, a few daffodils, and a trout plant just coming out, brilliant as the border in a tapestry. Against the wall on the terrace I did get the pansies in and now the blue windflowers are coming out.

I woke before six thinking of my mother who on this day sixty-seven years ago was determined to get strawberry plants in and went right on, lying down with labor pains then getting up to finish. I was born at ten-thirty in the evening after a hard labor, hard partly because the chauvinist brute of a doctor sat in an armchair with his feet up, smoking a cigar (!) and saying periodically "Poussez, Madame, poussez!" They brought her a bunch of lilies of the valley from the garden . . . today they are not yet in sight, but this is a late spring.

This is not quite like my sixty-fifth birthday when I was overjoyed, writing poems again after a long silence, a year of renewal. Now I am back in the valley of the shadow struggling along, but hopeful that seventy may be another vintage year, and this may be the year for patience, for rebuilding some loam from which flowers will grow in time.

This has been interrupted by a phone call from Lotte

Jacobi. She is eighty-four and in a year of glory, for everything that had been withheld when I first knew her twenty years ago or more is now flowering in her hands. I am sad to miss the first showing of a documentary film about her while I'm in England. What a blessing to hear her voice today!

Then Mary-Leigh and Beverly came with gifts of champagne and potpourri from Stourhead. How can I ever complain when I have such friends? I have been opening presents for days, one by one. Ann and Barbara come for dinner tonight, lobsters and strawberries in kirsch with whipped cream. I hulled the strawberries after breakfast. Dorothy Wallace, Rene Morgan, and Lenore Strauss all called before eight, and now dear Laurie.

But the fact remains that despite all this, if I were a dog I would sit and howl. It has been a year of endings. I opened *The Journals and Letters of the Little Locksmith,* a long out of print treasure that Ilse Vogel found for my birthday, to this message:

> I think the secret of much of the unrest and dissatisfaction with one's self and longing for a more vivid, expressive existence is the thing planted deep in everyone—turning toward the sun, the love of a virtue and splendor that must be adored. One has an inward sense of harmony. I mean one recognizes, by instinct, the celestial harmony and must try to adjust one's natural discord and dis-symmetry to match it. One is always trying to tune one's self to an unheard perfection.

Saturday, May 26th

HOME TO POURING RAIN and a rich green world here.
Tulips are over, cherries almost, but the lilacs are in full
bloom and scent the air in the rain. I have been on a real
holiday, far away for two weeks, on a barge on the
Thames, in London, and finally for a full week on the
island of Sark with Huldah. There we tasted the joys of
English spring, sitting in fields of bluebells and primroses
high up on the cliffs, looking down at the lazy gulls floating
the air currents far below. The air was full of birdsong,
linnets, thrushes, and finches flying up from the hedge-
rows as we walked past, and listened for the cuckoo far off
in another field. For two weeks we immersed ourselves in
simply being, a time of peaceful unhurried explorations.
The tempo on Sark is one of its charms, the tempo of
walking, since there are no cars.

Now real life charges in again with about one hundred
letters piled up, and this week both Karen Saum for one
day and Martha and Marita for four days to continue with
their respective video tape and filmed interviews with me
here. Apparently it has rained for two weeks. I did not
miss the spring here after all, since there was none, only
wetness and wild. I'm still on English time, wake at four,
get up at five, much to the delight of Tamas who rushes
out into the howling wind, barking.

Monday, May 28th

RAIN AGAIN, but I did manage three hours in the garden yesterday at last—sowed nasturtiums and calendulas, planted a row of marigold plants near where the tomatoes will be, cleaned out the delphinium choked with weeds and witch grass, cut out a huge bundle of dead clematis on the fence, pruned the climbing roses. It felt good but I came in at six daunted by how much should be done in the next days, eighteen or more annuals still to be sown and tomorrow Karen comes for a day's video-tape shooting and Thursday Martha and Marita for the main work, four days, on their filmed interview. The only thing to do is "one at a time," take each day as it comes and not think ahead to the next.

When I went down at six this morning I found maggots in the garbage pail, and all around it under the sink, the most repulsive sight imaginable. But it was rather satisfactory to get it all cleaned out and washed, and new plastic bags set under the pail. I love cleaning out and ordering, but no one could believe that who opened any cupboard or drawer in this house! If only I had three or four lives instead of one I could do better. Somehow the maggot encounter seemed an image of what coming home after a holiday is like, a clutter and intrusion of things that have to be done when what one needs is time to sort things out, to discover what has really happened, and very gently put down the fragile roots that sustain daily life.

Grackles have taken over the bird feeder, daunting even the squirrels. But yesterday I did catch a glimpse of the rose-breasted grosbeak, so delightful in his black and white with a half-moon crimson breast. The finches have disappeared.

Among the many letters I found here several suggest that I have made it clear that I hate getting letters. That is not it at all. Over the years the letters have given me the courage to go on, and not to despair. What is difficult is answering them all, not because I don't enjoy answering, but because there are so many; I never catch up.

Wednesday, May 30th

RAIN AGAIN. Since I've been back there have been only two afternoons when I could garden. Yesterday I got in five rows of seeds, blue salvia (a first try this year), zinnias, love-in-a-mist, annual chrysanthemums, and phlox. I also put in two big tomato plants and surrounded them with black plastic—at least there is no need to water anything! It's misting today, a drizzle, but the men are cutting the grass as it had begun to look like a field rather than a lawn. I pray that the weather will clear this weekend when Martha and Marita will be here.

I find it hard to think on this stiff spare typewriter. I hope my old trusty will soon be ready, then perhaps I can approach writing anything at all with a little more enthusiasm. It seems a long time since I have done any real work and I miss it, the continuity and rhythm under the days. But God knows when I shall be ready to have another try at a novel. I have a small seed in mind, but it has not begun to sprout, and only time will tell whether it ever will. I feel clogged by what is expected of me from the outside and for that reason far from the primary source. For that reason or some other reason I am having a series of nightmares. Yesterday it was that I came home to a small house with whitewashed walls (rather like the modest stone houses on Sark) to find that a skylight had been bashed in and every piece of furniture stolen . . . I had been cleaned out. It did not seem strange, but almost a relief to start again from scratch. Bill Brown had some similar dreams, he told me, repeated dreams of being thieved and his question now is, "Who is the thief?"

I used to be bored by dreams, my own or those of others, not inclined to pay attention to them as valid signposts or alerts, but Karen Buss sent me *The Dream Makers,* a book about break-through dreaming by two psychiatrists. I read it on Sark and found it convincing. No doubt what is buried tries to make its way through in dreams. But I have (I think) not had a censor around . . . I think I have let whatever happened flow in its own way through me. That has been a cause of acute pain at times, but the point is the flow, not to stop what is trying to be born. My worst fault is indiscretion and I believe that is because I do not have a normal censor. At least I have been able to face whatever is happening, to explore and use it, not to be afraid of the pain of *knowing.* People who turn away from what is happening and/or bury it are afraid of growing. At the perilous point where growth may be possible, there is an instinct to say "Stop! I don't want to know. It's too painful."

Friday, June 1st

AT LAST A SHINING DAY that looks as though it would stay, not darken into a shower for a change. I have the morning for myself before Martha and Marita start filming, a little unexpected gift of time in which to sort things out. The day before yesterday as I read the *Times* I came upon Marynia Farnham's obituary. It is a blessing to know that she has been allowed to go at last, after these last years when she did not recognize anyone, talked only to herself in a strange singing monotone, the words incomprehensible. Now the long decline can be forgotten and the rich snowy days can come back when I used to drive over to Winchester to drink champagne in her great room filled with works of art, listen to music, and talk. The real Marynia can come back into memory, her flashing dark eyes, her laughter, and her salty wisdom.

I had been very lonely in Nelson when I first met her, and I shall never forget walking into that big room the first time . . . I felt I had come home at last. This was after I had been her patient and we had begun to be friends. She seemed, with her whippets around her, like some lady in a tapestry. Unbelievable in the midst of the cultural poverty with which I was surrounded to be in the presence again of such a civilized life and ethos! Not since Edith Kennedy, who had been dead thirty years or more then, had I found a person with whom I could talk about everything in depth, and who could bring to our exchanges such a wide frame of reference. In that room I learned a great deal. For her I wrote many poems, a whole book that has never been published. Let me place two of them here, in memoriam.

A Birthday

This is a house inhabited
By Beatrix Potter, Mozart,
Gaston Lachaise,
A doll who offers a bunch of flowers
To the slow tinkle of a music box,
Two stuffed owls,
An old French clock—
A house full of good spells,
A house full of love,
Old and new,
Strange and simple,
Violent and merry.

And here in this magic house
Lives a passionate child
With great dark eyes,
A child who is also
A woman in her seventh decade,
A doctor of the human soul.

Three whippets and a white cat
Sleep on her bed.
Marynia wakes early
For fear of missing something—
Light on a single yellow leaf,
A scarlet tanager at the feeder,
Once a newborn donkey
Standing beside its mother.
Who knows what may happen
Early in the morning?

Marynia wakes
Before the telephone
Brings its weeping voices
Into the house.
One hand, large and gentle,
Strokes a dog's head
While she summons her wisdom,
Cuts woe down
With luminous reason,
Demands courage.

It has needed massive powers
Of light and compassion
To be so ready for instant response
Early in the morning
Or late at night.
But "I am always expecting a surprise,"
Marynia says.

She gets impatient
When nothing happens—
Better a cat up a tree
Than nothing at all.

"And what next?" Marynia asks,
"What's going to happen next?"

Right now
Hunca Munca is coming in with the cake.
Blow out the candles and make a wish.
That's what happens next.

"And after that?"
A journey, a book to write,
A new year, and always love,
Love knocking at the door.
Peter Rabbit tore his jacket
And will be very late.
Aunt Jemima could not get up the hill.

But we, some owls, a bear, and a bee,
We are here, you see,
To say, "Happy Birthday!
Happy New Year, Marynia!"
With hoots, hugs, and honey,
With love and ceremony.

The Place Beyond Action

In these airy balances
Between music and poetry
Between kinds of love
And kinds of deprivation,
How softly we must tread!
Of course you, secret person,
Learned long ago to walk the tightrope
Between attachment and detachment,
Learned never to stumble
On its perilous tension . . .

Nevertheless,
Attentive to a whisper,
I know your passion
And feel your violence.

Sometimes I love the somber person
Who rises up from a glass of wine
To curse the "cultural desert"
Where we both live,
God knows why.

Sometimes I hate the somber person
Who makes me feel like a desert
Where nothing can bloom,
For I am the prisoner
Of what I see
And can do nothing to change.

You are alone and should not be,
Rich Ceres, great giver,

That is the truth,
And it is hardly to be borne.
I bear it with an ill grace,
Trying to remember
Your valor, resilience,
The fertile mind,
The changing moods
Like clouds over a landscape
Of hills and lakes, light-shot,
Never at rest, expecting surprises.

In the airy balance
Where we sometimes achieve communion
It will always be possible
To move outside the deprivations,
Yours and mine,
Into a curious detached region
Natural to you, achieved by me,
That is music, that is poetry.
It is the place beyond action
And even sometimes beyond thought—
At worst unnatural
So much must be denied,
At best, nourishing,
So much has been accepted.

It all ended badly, because of senility, but what does that matter now? Now I can come back to the essence, and the essence was life-giving, and remains so.

While one stops to mourn the dead and to reapprehend their reality, life keeps bringing its new relations and marvelous passages where we witness growth in each other. The day I saw the obit in the *Times,* Jill Felman, my young writer friend, came to tea. For the past five years we have met at long intervals to revel in a long intimate dialogue about our work and our lives. I have watched Jill grow—she is twenty-five now I think. She is breaking through her Jewish heritage that seemed for a time both her richest source as a writer, and at the same time, a prison. She is breaking through into her real life as a caring woman who will probably not marry. I saw that in her and she saw in me at once, she said, some ease, some absence of tension, a recovery. I was surprised that she saw it so quickly . . . surprised and pleased. Jill is off to Israel for eleven weeks, excited on the edge of adventure, on the edge of doing good work.

Yesterday I got a haunting record of Japanese music for flute and harpsichord, with a letter in it from the Phoenix . . . so I call Dorothy Koeberlin who is battling increasing disability as a diabetic. Through letters I have known her for years, always refreshed and given courage by her courage, her acute sense of life as it is more and more taken from her. In this letter she says,

I had three transfusions but am still unable to walk, and oh, how I long for that. I can remember hot muggy days in Nebraska when the air sat upon me like a true burden. Then in the early evening the wind would come bringing with it delicately perfumed coolness off the fields where hay had been mown in the afternoon—it was like being resurrected. The spirit arose out of its stifling tomb and saw all things in a new and different light —it became alive. That is what I long for now—that sense of physical aliveness that pushes against the frame, enervates the flesh, that makes one feel as though even the skeletal mass is expanding and growing.

Today what joy to praise three marvelous women, and to rejoice that their paths have crossed mine.

Monday, June 4th

MARTHA AND MARITA and their crew, six men and women in all, have been here since Friday filming and recording. By great good luck the first three days gave us ideal filming weather, dry and cool with lovely light splashing through leaves on the walk through the woods, and one section of interview outside on the terrace where the wisteria is at perfection. Otherwise it's an in-between season here, the greens still fresh and brilliant, but no flowers until the azaleas and rhododendron come out, then iris and peonies.

It has been a joyous experience for me to be present and watch how the group works together and with what delicacy and consideration they have treated me. Of course we have been working on tiny segments, half an hour to set cameras up for a minute's walk with Tamas, so it's not possible yet to imagine what it will all look like in the end. I feel sure that the surroundings will come through like a poem, but am less certain about my part in it. One difficulty is that there is such a large body of work involved, how to choose what is most important, also which poems to read. Martha and Marita have managed, in spite of their necessary preoccupation with technical matters and the minutiae of setting the scene, to create an atmosphere so appreciative that I have not felt self-conscious but able to transcend physical weight and old age, and to feel transparent and alive. I am grateful.

Among my birthday presents was a book on Indonesian and Sumatran textiles by Joseph Fischer. His wife, Clare, did much to organize my readings in Berkeley, and their house is a treasure house of Indonesian art. I find these designs unexpectedly moving because of the delicacy and intricacy of their variations on traditional themes and symbols. It came to my mind as I wrote to thank the Fischers this morning that this excitement of the individual playing with strict forms is very much like the excitement of the poet playing with traditional forms, or the infinite variations that a ballet dancer can create within the strict form of ballet steps.

One thing I have not managed to talk about in the film is why strict form in poetry still has value and always will. We forget, perhaps, that poetry began eons ago and was associated with dance. Meter is how the body still gets involved on the subconscious level. We no longer dance to poetry or as we listen to it, but way below the conscious level, the beat opens doors. Why when the beat is so much a part of popular music, does it seem "old-fashioned" to use it as a tool in poetry?

Tuesday, June 5th

THIS FROM Katharine Butler Hathaway's *Journal* I was reading last night,

But in spite of the fact that I have made a number of portraits in pencil, and believe really that I am improving, I have only done it halfheartedly. To-shihoko's disturbing presence has been like a paraly-sis on me. When he is coming in and out in all his varying moods, my instinct is always to be what I always was with him—a listener, a consoler, simply a woman; and this mood is utterly contrary to creative mood. If I am an artist, I am neither a man nor a woman. It is intense, impersonal, and nonhuman. It kills the impulse to go out toward him or any other man, I think.

The thing is that art doesn't brook a censor and in the relation to those we love if it is not a perfect harmony we have to censor ourselves, keep the demons at bay. Then censorship in one area ends by taking over all areas. I am plagued by bad memories of last summer and wake dragged down into that morass. Sometimes I wonder whether the ideal would not be to censor drastically the whole past and try at least to live absolutely in the present —on condition that there life is permitted to flow, and not censored at all. Whatever breaks or stops the flow even when the flow is grief or pain, ends by killing the soul. I look forward very much to a summer at home here, to letting myself live, uncensored. I have given up all I can afford to give up for the sake of others and their needs. I would like to feel wholly myself for a change . . . and in a subtle way the work on the interview has helped me to see that. Yesterday I read twelve poems for the film. The crew were so with me, that it was like being given back my deepest self. It was the way they listened, and even wept at one point. I felt lifted up and restored to all I have had to bury lately.

It is so long since I have felt loveable or even accept-able. And I had been afraid of the camera eye, that it would make me feel old and ugly, that I would feel too exposed. But that was to forget that Marita was behind the camera and Martha at her side. They knew how to look at me and to see me as I really am.

Wednesday, June 6th

THE SILENCE! At last I have it, now the crew has left and also the workmen who have been painting the trim on the house. There is no sound except the faint hush-hushing of waves and a few twitters of birds. The murmur of the ocean sounds low and deep today, a gentle roar a little like distant thunder. It is clear and cool and I look forward to gardening this afternoon, perhaps mulching the annual bed already teeming with tiny weeds.

Someone sent me Adrienne Rich's *Women and Honor; Some Notes on Lying.* She says,

An honorable human relationship—that is, one in which two people have the right to use the word 'love'—is a process, delicate, violent, often terrifying to both persons involved, a process of refining the truths they can tell each other.

It is important to do this because it breaks down human self-delusion and isolation.

It is important to do this because in so doing we do justice to our own complexity.

It is important to do this because we can count on so few people to go that hard way with us.

Because passionate love breaks down walls and at first does it in such a sovereign way, we are rarely willing to admit how little that initial barrier-breaking is going to count when it comes to the slow, difficult, accepting of each other, when it comes to the irritations and abrasions, and the collisions, too, between two isolated human beings who want to be joined in a lasting relationship. So the walls go up again. The moment's vision is clouded, and mostly, I believe, by the fear of pain, our own and that of the other's, by the fear of rejection. To be honest is to expose wounds, and also to wound. There is no preventing that. Union on a deep level is so costly that it very rarely takes place. But withdrawal, censorship, the wish to keep the surfaces smooth because any eruption spells danger and must therefore be prevented, is costly also. Censorship simply drives conflict deeper inside. What is never discussed does not for that reason cease to exist. On the contrary, it may fester and finally become a killing poison.

Thursday, June 7th

IN WESTERN CULTURE, since the Renaissance anyway, we have sometimes been unwilling to face the destructive side of Eros. Sometime last August there was a review in the *Times Literary Supplement* (how I miss it now that the *Times* of London is no more!) of a book by John Boardman and Eugenio La Rocca called *Eros in Greece*. The review is by W. B. Stanford and yesterday, I remembered it and found it again. It struck me with great force. Here are excerpts:

> Ideas and images of Eros as a god and as a passion varied widely in ancient Greece, ranging from the highly idealistic to the grossly bestial. . . .
>
> But when he was first described as a god, by Hesiod, he was one of the three primordial beings of the cosmos, with Chaos and Earth. (Aphrodite came into existence several aeons later.) By the end of the pagan period he had become trivialized as an infantile cupid or sentimentalized by romance writers or animalized by pornographers. Only Plato's doctrine that the passion of *eros* could be a means of ascent to the Celestial Forms—'the desire and pursuit of the Whole'—offered a unifying doctrine to idealists who sought some higher meaning in this half-divine, half-bestial passion.
>
> There is one major difficulty in any discussion of *eros* as a passion. The English language offers no quite satisfactory equivalent for it. Boardman renders it as 'love', but to do so without any explanation or qualification may be misleading. Though the two words have much in common, they can differ radically in tone and scope. 'Love' usually implies pleasure or kindness.
>
> In contrast, *eros* appeared to many Greeks as a dangerous and disruptive force, compelling even right-minded people to do foolish, humiliating and painful things. This *eros* is sometimes described as a disease or madness with distressing symptoms and effects and not as something to be enjoyed. . . .
>
> Clearly then, Eros was not always regarded as a pleasurable experience by the Greeks. Nor had the Greeks any illusions about the selfishness and self-centeredness of the passion that Eros inspired. . . .

When they wanted to describe affection between parents and children or between friend and friend they used other words. The word *eros* essentially meant passionate desire to possess and enjoy, with no implication of tenderness.

For most of us Eros is an earthquake. There is fear and trembling and, above all, radical change involved . . . it is quite foolish to deny that our sexuality is deeply disturbing at any age. And most of us have a built-in censor to deal with this—too bad. On the other hand to pretend that Eros is not a primordial being of the same order as Earth and Chaos is to trivialize or screen off what has to be faced and experienced if we are to come into our humanity as whole beings, and if we are to reach Agape. Perhaps every serious love affair is the reexperiencing of history—psychic history.

Friday, June 8th

SAW DR. DOW YESTERDAY, and, as I have suspected for some time, I shall be going into the York hospital on the seventeenth for a biopsy, followed at once, Dr. Dow believes, by a mastectomy of the left breast. It is no surprise, and in some ways a relief, for I know that the amount of suppressed rage I have suffered since last fall had to find some way out. I have always believed that my mother's cancer came from suppressed rage, and Dr. LeShan's findings after much work with cancer patients bear me out. I look on the operation as a kind of exorcism. Something had to give, as they say.

I am grateful that humane, wise Dr. Dow is allowing me to read poems in Camden on the fifteenth to raise money for the Shakespeare theatre there. After that I have no commitments to read poems for a year, and can recover quietly in this beautiful place.

Yesterday was like a dream of June, cool, clear, all the greens sparkling and the ocean deep blue, and quiet. I felt strangely happy all day.

I would have more to say but I must try to clear the desk, or all those voices begging for an answer will haunt me in the hospital. . . .

Tuesday, June 26th

THE OPERATION was on the eighteenth and I came home yesterday welcomed by dear Martha and Marita who have been holding the fort here.

The York hospital, small, intimate, and kind, was an ideal place for me to be, especially as I was on their new plan, Joint Practice, where nurses are given unusual powers and work closely with the surgeon. The operation was not bad at all, a modified radical mastectomy . . . modified meaning that they found no malignancy in the lymph glands. It looks as though I am in the clear.

I had a room of my own until the last night, and it was soon full of flowers, glorious flowers, among them a bunch of many sprays of delphinium, several blues, and white peonies. Another was a basket with six African violets of shades of pink and lavender. The first day Heidi brought a little bunch from her garden, and later on Martha and Marita brought me samples from my garden, one day two clematis, one deep purple and one white, another day, Siberian iris. The flowers were a constant joy. I opened my eyes to find them there, silent presences, and I slept a lot, grateful for the loss of consciousness.

The flowers helped, the visible sign of the love of many, many friends, and the great elm tree I looked at from the window helped too, its long branches waving gently in the wind. One evening an oriole came to rest there and sing. The changing skies and the admirable steadfast tree did me a lot of good. I needed it, for I had imagined that the loss of a breast would create catharsis, that I would emerge like a phoenix from the fire, reborn, with all things made new, especially the pain in my heart. I had imagined that real pain, physical pain, and physical loss would take the place of mental anguish and the loss of love. Not so. It is all to be begun again, the long excruciating journey through pain and rejection, through anger and not understanding, toward some regained sense of my self. I have in the past six months been devalued, as a woman, as a lover, and as a writer. How to build back to a sense of value, of valuing myself again?

At least I have proved that I have some resilience. Today I had a bath and changed the bandage myself, not without terror as a lot of fluid spurted out. But what bliss to sleep last night with Tamas and Bramble on each side of me!

Thursday, June 28th

PERHAPS THERE HAS BEEN a greater inward change than
I can yet measure, and if so, it has to do with the miracle
of human trust and lovingness that Martha and Marita
have created here for and with me. They are leaving
today. Yesterday they installed the air conditioner up
here, and we waited all day for the telephone company to
come and extend telephone cords so I can be saved from
getting up to answer calls. That will be a great help. They
have watered the garden, cooked a delicious dinner each
night, and we have had long talks about their lives and
hopes and mine, sometimes with tears flowing down our
cheeks. They say they are my family (they each have
living parents but this is something else, for it is they who
mother me though they are twenty years younger).

    It was very hard to ask Martha to come . . . she had
offered three times, had insisted that she would "come at
the drop of a hat" if needed. But she and Marita are just
settling in to a country place they have bought along the
Delaware River; they are hard at work putting the film
together; and Martha still has a lot to do on her thesis. I
hated to ask, but I did it finally when it was clear that
Karen, who was with me through the operation for the
first two days, would miss her California trip if she stayed
on. So I did ask, and the only hard thing about these days
was having to ask for help from the young. I should have

remembered what Jean Dominique taught me long ago, that accepting dependence with grace was one of the last lessons we all have to learn. With the help of such tact and understanding, it has turned out to be revelatory. Perhaps it is teaching me to bury the one-pointed heart, that fierce infant demand that there must be one person, my person, on whom I could and must depend. Perhaps it is teaching me to rest lightly on the palms of the many hands that have been lifting me so gently all these days, an ever present sense of thought flowing toward me. I felt when I went into the hospital that I was carrying with me an invisible bunch of flowers, each flower a dear friend.

Sunday, July 1st

NOT THE EASIEST OF TIMES, but I think I am doing well as a physical being at least. It is half past nine, and all night we had a much-needed rain so my anxiety about the parched garden can rest and that is a relief. Since seven I have got my breakfast and washed it up, washed the sheets and put fresh ones on my bed, fresh towels in the bathroom, a fresh dressing on my wound, went down cellar to put the lights on over seedlings down there, and now I am dressed and up here on the third floor for some hours of writing. The hardest thing is letters for the moment, as my head is worse off than my body these days. There appears to be very little psychic juice available— but then it is only thirteen days since the operation.

I have been thinking a lot about the body and what a miracle it is, the extraordinary summoning of aids and defenders and healers so hard at work now mending the big gash where my left breast was. The body is a universe in itself and must be held as sacred as anything in creation, as every miraculous bird and beetle and moth and tiger. It is dangerous to forget the body as sacramental . . . because the minute one does then mutilation, the mutilation of a wound, or simply the mutilation of old age can kill the spirit. An old body when it is loved becomes a sacred treasure; and sex itself must always, it seems to me, come to us as a sacrament and be so used or it is meaningless. The flesh is suffused by the spirit, and it is forgetting this in the act of love-making that creates cynicism and despair.

What I am fighting now is depression, but it is not, I think, wholly and perhaps at all, the result of the shock of a major operation on the body. The body can handle shock with amazing resilience. Shock calls out hidden powers.

It is that I feel devalued and abandoned at the center of my being. I sometimes feel that everyone else manages to grow up and harden in the right way to survive, whereas I have remained a terribly vulnerable infant. When poetry is alive in me I can handle it, use it, feel worthy of being part of the universe. When I can't, as now, when the source is all silted up by pain, I think I should have been done away with at birth. Absurd overreacting to the loss of love.

Monday, July 2nd

I HAVE BEEN THINKING about that baby in me who has
tantrums and cries, trying to accept that it and the wise
old woman whom I am at times are part of a single whole.
And I have been thinking also that twice in my life people
who discovered me through the work, who came to me
as admirers and became intimate friends ended by being
unable to accept the whole person, the flawed human
being because they had somehow fallen in love with an
image beside which the reality of a living, suffering being
who is not perfect, who is temperamental, who "has no
surface" as someone has said of me, became disillusioning.

And once more I turn for comfort to Florida Scott-
Maxwell's *The Measure of My Days,* and at once find this:

> There seems a widespread need of living and learn-
> ing the dark side of our nature. Perhaps we are al-
> most on the point of saying that evil is normal, in
> each of us, an integral part of our being. This age may
> be witnessing the assimilation of evil, thereby finding
> a new wisdom. We have been insisting for centuries
> that evil should not be, that it can be eliminated, is
> only the absence of good, resides in others; if others
> are evil, we are not, or so little that it hardly matters.
> Now we are fascinated by evil. Does it begin to be
> clear that it is half of life, and its extreme is truly evil?
> Are we learning that without the tension between
> good and evil there would be no dynamism in life?

Perhaps our two cruel wars were a climax of evil making us see a truth we have always fled. If this profound realization is taking place, then what seems our decadence may be the stirring of a new reality, even a new morality, God willing and man able.

What a perilous morality. Will humanity ever be equal to it? Where will the difference lie between the man who blindly lives his chaos, and the man who consciously endures the conflict between opposing sides of his nature? The latter will gain clarity, a deepened awareness, and he will achieve responsibility for many aspects of his being, but much of the time the two men will look the same.

How that last sentence makes me ponder!

These days I feel often on the brink of revelation. Last night I lay awake from one to about four, so full of life and intentions and ideas I felt immense power flowing through me like an electric current. It may be that overcoming does literally bring new strength. But this morning I am paying for the sleepless hours. I see, but I haven't the strength to write it all down.

Thursday, July 5th

I'VE BEEN OVERDOING and have lost the shining thread of energy that I spoke of the other day. Ann and Barbara came for dinner on Monday, bringing the salad from their garden and doing all the work for me, but over four hours of intense communication (how dear and how welcome it

was!) took it out of me and unfortunately two charming
fans from California and New York had invited me out to
dinner the following night. I enjoyed them immensely,
and also having a bang-up July 4th dinner of salmon and
fresh peas from her garden at Heidi's yesterday, my first
drive of some distance. But today I am a miserable rag
with an attack of diverticulitis and no margin of energy
left at all. Perhaps I'll just lie down and sleep for an hour,
now the chores are done and I am dressed. Then I can
walk Tamas, get the mail, and maybe climb up by afternoon to a small peak from which to survey the world with
a little more zest.

Friday, July 6th

I NEVER DID REACH a small peak of energy yesterday but
slept a deep sleep from one to five in the afternoon and
I guess that was what the old body was crying out for, for
today I am much better and expect to be quite fit enough
to take Tamas to Wells tomorrow morning to be washed
and combed. That looms as quite an effort, but the poor
dear is a thicket of tangled fur and will suffer when the hot
days come if I don't get it done now.

This morning I dragged the hose to where it could
reach the young chrysanthemums—everything is dry as a
bone, but who could complain about such weather? Clear
and cool and just dandy. The strange self-sown poppies
that have been in the picking garden since I came and
may be opium poppies are coming into flower, a glowing

pink. They look splendid beside some tall sprays of dark purple and white delphinium. Otherwise there is nothing yet to pick, but any day now the Japanese iris will come out, and then lilies, so the garden is filled with expectation.

Joy Sweet came to see me in the hospital and spent the night here with Martha and Marita. I found a note from her when I came home with a passage in it from Rilke that has been haunting me. "Once the realization is accepted that even between the closest human beings infinite distances continue to exist, a wonderful thing side by side can grow up, if they succeed in loving the distance between them which makes it possible for each to see the other whole against the sky."

That is surely an ideal vision, but I suspect that Rilke was one of those for whom distance is actually necessary, one of those who cannot cope with intimacy, who is destroyed by it or too dispersed by it to feel fully himself. Whereas he was able to encompass "the other" with extraordinary sensitivity at a distance, and through letters.

What I long for with those I love is not so much to be understood as to be accepted warts and all, to feel safe to be fully myself even when there are great temperamental differences. What I mean by feeling "safe" is to know that I shall not be cast out when I cry or am angry, to be in the deep sense acceptable because it has been understood that the violence has its positive side.

I have sometimes felt in this past year that I have become at least for one person important to my inner life, a carrier of the plague . . . the plague being feelings. She herself is so afraid of feeling, or her own feelings, as though they were a dangerous tide that might engulf her, that she has come to see me as the enemy, the master of this tide she cannot bear because it frightens her too much. So she barricades herself against me and in my turn I feel devalued, made into nothing, unacceptable, the carrier of the plague.

"Teach us to care, and not to care"—all very well, but in human relations where intimacy is involved, it may be that when we have achieved detachment, the relationship itself will come to seem hardly worth the immense effort of imagination it has cost to sustain it, and the pain involved in trying to bridge the distance.

Sunday, July 8th

RENE MORGAN came unexpectedly overnight and in twenty-four hours did things I have contemplated for months and might not have achieved in a year, to wit reorganizing kitchen cupboards so the dog and cat food no longer clutter up a counter, and half a dozen other such deeds, including helping me drag the hoses around, for we need rain. When Rene left yesterday afternoon I, as always when help has been abounding, felt scared about how to cope, but I did manage to change the hoses around (the first time I've had the strength because uncoupling requires a twist of the arm that hurt too much). This morning I woke up trying to remember Yeats' "Song of a Fool":

> A speckled cat and a tame hare
> Eat at my hearthstone
> And sleep there;

And both look up to me alone
For learning and defence
As I look up to Providence.

I start out of my sleep to think
Some day I may forget
Their food and drink;
Or, the house door left unshut,
The hare may run till it's found
The horn's sweet note and the tooth of the hound.

I bear a burden that well might try
Men that do all by rule,
And what can I
That am a wandering-witted fool
But pray God that he ease
My great responsibilities?

Yesterday I did take Tamas to be washed and combed,
a drive of three-quarters of an hour each way, which I had
to do twice to fetch him after noon—how much energy
the usual tasks that keep life going here, actually use up!
But Tamas is so fluffy, sweet-smelling, and burnished that
it was well worth the effort. He and I slept the sleep of the
just last night, both exhausted, while Bramble stayed out
under the full moon.

One of the insights that has come to me through the
operation is that physical disability rouses the will, so
much so that extra power seems to be given in overcoming it, power beyond what is needed. (I think of Roosevelt
for instance after the attack of polio.) Whereas depression,
mental anguish, destroy the will or numb it. So they are
much harder to handle. I sometimes wonder whether I
shall ever fully recover the sense of myself and of my
powers as a writer and as a person after last year. It is as
though the central psychic motor had been damaged.
When shall I be able to rev it up again to full speed ahead?

Tuesday, July 10th

I AM HAPPY to hear that Judy's family, so sensitive to her needs, so much on the job, came to the decision two weeks ago or more, to move her to a smaller nursing home where she is in a less institutional atmosphere. Connie, her sister, went to see her around two one day and found her eating strawberry shortcake with evident relish, sitting in her wheelchair in the parlor there. The best news is that she is now off tranquilizers (overused no doubt in the larger place) and as soon as I can drive that far, I long to see her, and perhaps to erase my last vision of her some months ago, sitting alone in her room, her face turned away, with a look of tragic emptiness in it. I have thought of Judy so much since the operation, benign star in my firmament, she who could and did love me for what I am and accepted the flaws. The never-failing support and friend.

Yesterday Morgan Mead came, bearing lunch, vichyssoise he had made himself and delicious ham sandwiches. We had, as always, so much to talk about that the two hours went too fast. The great joy of being with the young is that they are still growing. Morgan is full of a rare tenderness toward life, and I am happy to hear him say he would like to marry. He longs to be a father, but also he has a great compassionate love of women, wants to help them . . . how rare! He went off with *Happy All The Time*, one of the few charming novels I have read in years (Laurie sent it to me). When he heard about the operation he said he went into shock and he wrote me the one letter that moved me to tears because he said in it, "I need you and I love you."

I am thinking of making a list of things *not* to say to someone recovering from surgery and in a weak state. One of them is surely "count your blessings"—as though one didn't, and as though to discount tragedy. Another is to emphasize that millions of women have had the same problem like saying to a child who has fallen and torn a knee open, "hundreds of children do this every day." You can't lump people together in a large inchoate mass, for that is to diminish each one's selfhood. No two loves are alike, no two deaths, and no two losses: these are paths we travel alone.

What the mastectomy does to each individual woman is, at least temporarily, to attack her womanhood at its most vulnerable, to devalue her in her own eyes as a woman. And each woman has to meet this and make herself whole again in her own way. (It is much harder, I feel sure, for a young woman for obvious reasons.)

The person who never says the wrong thing is Heidi. She has been the most supportive friend possible through all this.

Monday, July 16th

HULDAH HAS BEEN HERE for two days, unluckily enough
during a sudden heat wave, so it was heroic of her to work
in the garden. She did do two or three big jobs, clipping
and weeding, so what I look out on from the *chaise longue*
is orderly. It makes a big difference to my state of mind,
and altogether her brief visit gave me a lift.

Now the house feels empty; the silence is too silent.
There has been fog since she left which spares me from
watering, yet it feels like limbo here. Inspired by Huldah
I did a little weeding myself yesterday afternoon, but it
was a mistake as my left arm ached all night and still does.
Again I have leaped ahead too fast and must be patient.
But it is hard to be patient when the weeds shoot up in
such profusion and one knows that the longer one waits,
the harder it will be.

Wednesday, July 18th

I AM GOING THROUGH a rather low struggle, by that I mean that I am feeling an ebbing of that exhilaration I knew immediately after the operation when I was amazed and delighted at the body's powers of recovery, and it seemed miraculous to feel as well as I did. Also weakness, the need to lie down frequently, the necessity to "put off" chores and letters created a certain inner freedom simply to be. Now the weeds are there, growing apace, and the letters pile up and the real struggle to recover, maintain, and go on begins in earnest.

After that first attempt at weeding and two sleepless nights because of the aching arm, I went to see the doctor yesterday. He was reassuring, is pleased by my progress, and told me I simply have to pace myself like an athlete, not do too much, but on the other hand press on and sometimes pay for an effort that can do no harm. I was frankly afraid that I might be pulling my arm to bits. But on the strength of Dr. Dow's good advice I went out and tackled the horrendous weeds in the picking garden yesterday afternoon. A half hour was enough. Then I had the reward of picking a brilliant bunch of the first orange and yellow calendulas and mixing them with bright pink and red sweet peas, a rather Mexican mixture of colors. It was reviving.

I have not felt like writing in this journal. It lies in wait each morning, and I long to put it off. But today I'll give

myself courage by copying another passage from Florida
Scott-Maxwell whose book I never open without a shock
of recognition. (*The Measure of My Days,* page twenty-
one.) This time it was this passage that hit me hard:

> The ordeal of being true to your own inner way must
> stand high in the list of ordeals. It is like being in the
> power of someone you cannot reach, know, or move,
> but who never lets you go; who both insists that you
> accept yourself and who seems to know who you are.
> It is awful to have to be yourself. If you do reach this
> stage of life you are to some extent free from your
> fellows. But the travail of it. Precious beyond valuing
> as the individual is, his fate is feared and avoided.
> Many do have to endure a minute degree of unique-
> ness, just enough to make them slightly immune
> from the infection of the crowd, but natural people
> avoid it. They obey for comfort's sake the instinct
> that warns, 'Say yes, don't differ, it's not safe.' It is not
> easy to be sure that being yourself is worth the trou-
> ble, but we do know it is our sacred duty.

Lately I have been unusually unreceptive to the demands of people I do not know but who know me through
the books . . . and who expect, even demand, response
from me on a deep level. I used to feel that I had a responsibility to answer always, and for years such answers have
eaten into creative energy to a point that has become
impossible. For more than a year now I appear to have
been fighting for myself, fighting to recover the creative
being in me, fighting in essence to stay alive, not to become silted down in "obligations" that are escapes from
the far harder obligations to write poems and books. And
fighting too, against someone I love who is afraid of the
essential creative being and its daimons. The operation
has opened the way to my becoming an ornery character

who does not answer everyone and who does not allow guilt to enter the picture on that ground. The problem is that that is negative. The positive, opening of the door back into poetry that would justify it, has not happened. Will it ever again?

Saturday, July 21st

THERE ARE GREAT PLEASURES in not feeling well—I get up shockingly late for me, around seven-thirty, but Tamas wants to go out about six-thirty so I get up, and then go back to bed for a heavenly hour when, half asleep, I listen to the morning sounds, a faint murmur of ocean, the twittering musical garlands of the goldfinches in flight, the wood pigeons' repeated coos, and the low "frahnk" of the blue heron as he flies to the pond. The silence here is a very alive silence, but how incredible to wake in a room where there is no sound of machines of any kind . . . once in a long while the Coast Guard helicopter roars over on its rounds and occasionally a fighter plane from Pease Air Force Base. Otherwise the only mechanical sound is the gentle chug of the lobster boats early each morning.

It is so silent that I hear the cat's footsteps on the stairs.

The picking garden is choked with weeds, but it is also beginning to give me sweet joys . . . the calendulas are in flower. Those bright oranges and yellows, the satiny freshness of the petals as soft as birds' feathers and as beautifully arranged, have brought new life into the house these hot humid days when all colors except these look washed out. The lilies are beginning and the big saffron yellow day lilies, too. And I have had small bunches of roses in a little bowl by the *chaise longue* every day. We did get some rain two or three days ago, but now I must begin hauling the hoses around again. It does not involve stooping which is still difficult, and I enjoy it. Is there a greater pleasure than giving drink to the thirsty? It satisfies some atavistic need to take care and the very thought of thirsty roots drinking is reviving to the spirits.

Other recent joys have been a darling letter from a ninety-two-year-old woman who has been reading *The House By The Sea,* is full of life and able to cope in spite of the loss of her dear friend of sixty years. I wonder why it is that letters from the very old and from the very young give me the most pleasure. In the first instance perhaps because it is good to be younger than someone whom one can please, and in the second because it is good to be much older and still able to connect. In the hospital one of the odder things that happened was that I repeatedly woke thinking I was fifty-seven years old, amazed to think I had survived that long, only to realize with a shock that I am actually sixty-seven, ten years older than seems possible! It has been ground into me by the bitter experiences of last year that I am old, that I must be denied some things, that the door has closed forever on passionate communion with another human being. The mutilated body appears then to be the physical evidence of that fact. But the phoenix rising again from the flames tells me otherwise. The more our bodies fail us, the more naked and more demanding is the spirit, the more open and loving we can become if we are not afraid of what we are and of what we feel. I am not a phoenix yet, but here among the ashes, it may be that the pain is chiefly that of new wings trying to push through.

Monday, July 23rd

Epitaph for Everyman

My heart was more disgraceful, more alone,
And more courageous than the world has known.
O passer-by, my heart was like your own.

HOW OFTEN I go back to Frances Cornford, and her rare
succinct lyrics. I admire them more than I can say for they
make the unbearable bearable by their *art*, and that
surely is one of the functions of poetry. Not able to write
myself these days I am reading poems a lot. They make
me long to be filled with the great wind again.

But the epitaph came to my mind for another reason;
the whole question of ethos and why I believe that it is
good not bad to show feeling, and to admit failure. There
is another view, the British, and the puritanical one which
places human dignity in the highest place and which fundamentally believes that to show feeling is to admit weakness, to be in essence "undignified." There is much to be
said for this view. It makes for stern self-discipline, for not
"giving way" to tears, the stiff upper lip that can indeed
suggest heroism, the soldier dying with a joke on his lips.
(Still, there are heroes who knew better Nelson's "Kiss
me, Hardy " comes to mind at once.) Split as I am between my Belgian and English inheritance I see both
sides. I understand very well the British contempt for the
"frogs," those French who talk so much so excitedly and

burst into tears at a parade. And there is all the popular mythology and the sayings like "still waters run deep," that imply that silence is strength and hence that speaking out honestly is weakness. I wonder. When I think back on the people who have influenced me most and who were great for one reason or another—Lugné-Poë, Edith Kennedy, Jean Dominique, Koteliansky, Virginia Woolf, Elizabeth Bowen, Juliette Huxley, and nearer home Mildred Quigley, Perley Cole —they were all people of immense dignity and courage, but also they were all extremely articulate, not afraid of feeling and of expressing feeling. The exceptions are Anne Thorp and Grace Eliot Dudley, both New Englanders, both, curiously enough Francophiles. Their reserve was bred into the bone, and was an intrinsic part of their strength. And so it can be. But I believe it to be true that "still waters" may run shallow, not deep, and it is not always a sign of the facile in a pejorative sense to be articulate and to wish to give oneself away.

I would like to believe when I die that I have given myself away like a tree that sows seeds every spring and never counts the loss, because it is not loss, it is adding to future life. It is the tree's way of being. Strongly rooted perhaps, but spilling out its treasure on the wind.

Friday, July 27th

THE HEAVY HUMID WEATHER goes on and on. We had
rain all night and thunder and I had imagined we would
wake to a clear washed blue sky at last. Instead fog closed
in again. One feels weighed down as though by lead in the
bones. Up here in my study I have the air conditioner on.
It gives me a strange sensation of being totally isolated as
I'm insulated up here from all sounds except that mechanical rushing air from the window. A Mozart quintet airs
things out a bit, too.

My first overnight guests since the operation left an
hour ago. Ellen Hildebrand lives in South Carolina so we
meet very rarely, not for ten years this time. But she is a
real friend. The house is full of things she has made me
over the years, and we have each leaned on each other by
telephone in times of stress. What a joy to welcome her
and her friend, Eleanor, here, and to bask in the love and
understanding between these two grandmothers! We had
an orgy of good talk last night and were even able during
a brief respite when a breeze from the ocean sprang up,
to sit on the terrace for an hour before supper.

Now I have written postcards to three people who
deserve letters . . . a nurse in Colorado who works with the
dying and who says, "Your honesty and willingness to
share who you are have been—I can only say—redemp-
tive." The second from a young woman in California who
had been relieved to read of a woman's love for a woman

in *A Reckoning*. And the third from a woman in Tampa, Florida who charmed me by saying "The sounds of the words you choose, *your* words . . . many nights when I am worried or can't sleep, I take your books out on my back steps, and sit by my geraniums and the clothes line and read—poems, pages, paragraphs—out loud, simply to hear them, the sound of the words. And all they mean."

Isn't it enough to hear such things, to know the works have landed here or there across the country? Yes, it is enough. And I am in better spirits today than I have been for a long time.

Tuesday, July 31st

I HAVE BEEN SILENT because I have been working hard to get the book of poems arranged in a final form and revised. Sue Hilsinger and Lois Brynes vetted the manuscript ages ago, and made a lot of small suggestions. It is enormously helpful to be queried and hence make a new effort long after a poem has been written. It brought it all alive again for me. I carried single lines in my head like puzzles to solve when I was driving or washing dishes. Yesterday it was how to find the right adjective to replace "radiant" in describing a smile.

Of course this book is a huge risk . . . what book of mine has not been? It is a risk because these are pure lyrics. Nothing could be more unfashionable. But the fact is that the simple lyric is the rarest and most precious kind of poem as far as I am concerned. These are the poems that reach the greatest spontaneity and in this instance are very simple, using the simplest words. They are not at all clever, and maybe are a kind of "Old Woman's Garden of Verses," resembling Stevenson's "Child's Garden of Verses". The risk is also that it may seem absurd for an old woman to publish a book of simple love poems. But of course the answer to that is that true love makes us ageless, sends us back to primary emotion, as pure and naked as though it were the first love, not the last. What a miracle!

Once I really got going I could forget that the experience from which they came has changed and gone through hard times like dense thickets, and that I probably shall never again feel as I did. I got back to the sense that the poems are authentic, a record of something valid, something that did happen, and that happens to many people of all ages and sexes. I began to believe in them again.

I have been meaning to speak about Dorothy Bryant who gathered together a group of women for a long evening's talk when I was in Berkeley last April—we have become friends. With her novel, *The Kin of Ata Are Waiting For You*, she overcame my distrust and even dislike of fantasy in fiction (Madeleine L'Engle had been the exception until now). She had a hard time with the regular publishers in New York and after waiting months for a response on one of her novels decided to go it alone and with the help of her husband founded ATA Books in order to publish herself. What might look like an act of self-immolation is proving to open doors, and her work is getting the kind of recognition it might not have had in the welter of the thousands of novels the regular publishers bring out every year, five thousand or more, and which get lost in the shuffle. Recently there was a piece

in *Publishers Weekly* about Dorothy's successful venture
on her own. I must quickly say that this is a very different
matter than the unsuccessful writer who ends by paying
a vanity press simply to see herself or himself in print.
That is always a mistake. Dorothy embarked on publishing herself only after *Ata* had been published by Random
House. She had "made it" through the regular channels
but she began to see how little the regular channels help,
what a roulette game it has become, where a thousand
books are buried so that one "best seller" can be pushed.
By simply avoiding the horrors of "the media" Dorothy is
getting her work to the people. I can only say "Bravo!"

We have never had such a long run of humid heat
since I moved to Maine, no cool East wind to blow the
miasma away. It does make one feel curiously belea-
guered, especially because it is bug weather. While we are
dimmed, they thrive. I cannot go out without being attacked by clouds of mosquitos, so even picking raspberries
(such a treat!) becomes an ordeal and I have given up
trying to take Tamas on the walk through the woods because of the vicious deer flies. It doesn't help that hornets
have built one of their paper nests just below the terrace.
It was discovered the other day when Raymond got badly
stung while pruning the ubiquitous wild roses that move
into every cranny in this garden. His right eye swelled up
until he could hardly see, and his right arm also. I was
quite frightened.

It makes me cross not to be able to pick flowers in
peace. The zinnias are splendid now and the calendulas,
bachelor's-buttons, and nicotiana in the picking garden.
But then if I do pick a bunch it fades in a day or so.
Apparently there is no relief in sight, and I dream of
October, sharp air, and dark blue sea. It will come!

Thursday, August 2nd

THERE IS A NEW SOUND, the sound of high summer, the crickets in the grass. They sing their short chirring refrain all night, the only welcome insect these days, but they are welcome. It is a sound as soothing as distant surf, and puts me to sleep. Last night was breathless, even after quite a severe thunderstorm, but in our present hell here the storms do not clear the air, but only make it damper and heavier. Around three a.m. I feel I can't breathe and put the big fan on. It blows Tamas's fur and cools me off so I can pull up a sheet.

I don't know whether it is the effect of the operation but I am feeling rather domestic these days. I finally got someone to come and measure for new curtains in my bedroom and went into Portsmouth to choose the material some days ago. I love the old curtains that I inherited when I moved here, but they are falling to pieces and begin to look too shabby even for my tastes. I hate things that look too new, and realized at once that a blue and white stripe I had imagined might do (Margeson's did have it) would be much too bright and definite. Smart but not livable. I chose instead a soft flowery pattern in faded blues and browns. It keeps the feeling of the house and I like to think that Anne Robert would approve. Later I shall have a blue wall-to-wall rug put down. Tamas is terrified of slipping on the hardwood floors and sometimes stays on the threshold and won't come in to go to bed. Now that I can't lift him, it presents a problem.

Friday, August 3rd

MY MOTHER'S BIRTHDAY. And for the first time since her death twenty-nine years ago (is that possible?) I have opened the folders of letters and read some of her letters to me. I have dreaded doing this for years but instead of grief, they have brought me deep joy, a reaffirmation of our relationship, which was so rare in its freedom, as though we were intimate friends rather than mother and daughter. For my birthday when I was thirty-one she wrote me a little note,

Dear heart, I thought of you last night—remembering the hour you were born and the lovely day I had spent in the garden sowing seeds and hiding my pains (which were not bad until much later). I was beautifully alone in the kitchen garden and could curl up on the mossy path in the warm sun till the pain passed and then go right ahead! And I so wondered if you would be a boy or a girl and what you would be like: would you be very intelligent like Daddy and perhaps have little use for me when you grew up? And so on, endlessly, but not painfully. (I wasn't *really* afraid of you) it was a dreamy wondering and with a warm secret conviction that you would be very close to me whatever and whoever you proved to be . . . and I was right, wasn't I? and I haven't held you too tight, dear Pigeon, have I? because I do count freedom as among the most precious things in the world . . . and so have always wanted it for you.

Facing page Mabel Sarton with May at six months

And in the autumn of that year she sent me another memory,

Well, May darling, autumn is softly but definitely installed in Channing Place this morning—every sort of damp smell comes in at the open window. There is a dripping sound though it no longer rains, but the mist is so heavy it concentrates on ends of leaves and some it pulls down with the clear drop. The ground, which is dark and rain-soaked, is strewn with first-fallen leaves of such lovely and varied colors you would go out and make 'a collection' if you were four years old again. Do you remember those 'collections'? which we spread on the round table at 10 Avon Street? You went out and brought back more and more, each lovelier than the last as you became more difficult in your search for 'beauties'. You were eager and excited, and so was I, as if they were fabulous jewels suddenly, magically strewn in the streets for our delight and I think it added a strange and perhaps selfish little surprised joy that most other people did not recognize their value and their beauty. I am still stopped in the street by maple leaves,—the first, strewn sparsely, so one sees a pattern like the ones in my little Japanese book—their flower-reds from crimson through vermilion to carmine-pink and purest yellow-orange. They still make me give a little inward gasp of joy. There were some yesterday along Channing Street but no little girl collecting them . . . however she lives in my heart safely and gaily so who cares, and I, like you, meet her there from time to time.

In June of that year, mother had decided to have a tonsillectomy, to do it when both Daddy and I were away, with Anne Thorp to take her to the hospital and be with her through the hard time. She wrote me four days later in pencil.

O my darling, they're out and I'm *here,* safe in our quiet home, my windows filled with greenery against a delicate flower-blue sky, Daddy's kind eyes smiling at me from the door, as he retires to his study, a little bewildered by all this (and so taking refuge by taking *in* and putting *out* the cats!)

You went with me to the hospital (Hans's two photos). I waved my hand to you as they wheeled me out to go, and I saw you and Daddy with kittens in his arms, the first thing I *could* see deliberately when coming out of the ether. Then sixteen hours of hell, but it's over and it's much better than heaven to be here again. The doctors were swift, efficient, and infinitely kind. They have let me come home on the fourth day on my promise to stay in bed and *see no one.* I am still so tired, but that will pass. My throat hurts if I talk. I have to drive Mrs. C. away but in all other ways she is an angel.

Anne was my mainstay. Write her a loving word of thanks. She took me and stayed an hour Tuesday afternoon. Then she was telephoned to on Wednesday and was responsible for telling Daddy—not an easy responsibility. He was in New York but returned Thursday (by boat). Anne met him here at home and he came to see me twice that day. I do not yet know if he approves but I am so sure that I was right that I can't worry about it. He left the entire responsibility of the decision to me —made no attempt to get the Doctor's reasons, so I had to take that responsibility and felt I must spare him the dreadful hours that precede and follow an operation. He was much more frightened and doubtful *in a way* than I was, and could not hide it. It was not easy for me to do as I did, but I felt it was best for both of us. It's usually a very unimportant operation, but there were complications for me.

The garden is a mass of flowers—your irises you gave me are a glory of blue and purple and strange wine-red and still some clear greenish-white ones, loveliest of all.

A letter from you awaited me on my desk as I came in yesterday. O, my darling, I am no longer anxious and unhappy about you. It seemed to fall away from me, facing this ordeal— as something not truly important. I felt you radiant and clear beside me and blessed you as I bless you now.

Saturday, August 4th

THE WHOLE DAY yesterday was a celebration. After a rest
that afternoon I went out into the garden and picked a
sumptuous bunch of red and gold and orange calendulas,
zinnias, and one or two crimson cosmos and white
nicotiana, and then a little bowl of raspberries, thinking
all the time of my mother and the joy she would feel if she
knew I am in such a beautiful place, thinking of her not
so much as my mother but as herself, a unique human
being. The letters show her endless struggle against ill
health but everyone who knew her thought of her always
as a vivid, life-enhancing person, never as "frail" or often
ill as she was, and that in itself is wonderful to contem-
plate. Where did that fresh spring of courage and joy that
never went dry come from? Rosalind Greene wrote to my
father when she died, "The truth of her nature gave out
an undimmed light—and all her love of beauty, and of
persons, was made poignant by this imperishable integrity." Her strength came from very deep and had nothing
to do with discipline or control. She never became a character, set in her ways, but remained to the end a nature,
rich and open to life, able to deal with radical change and
to welcome it.

One thing happened yesterday that seems a miracle,
a release at last from a long bondage, for I have been
perhaps too aware for too long that, in spite of all I was
able to do for Mother in the last months, I failed in one

way that I cannot forget, that has haunted me all these
years. One day she asked me to sit with her for a while,
and I said "I can't" and rushed out of the room in tears.
Much of what I tried to suggest in *A Reckoning* about just
that need for someone to be there in silence, and perhaps
to speak out of the silence, came from this hard haunting
memory of what I myself failed to do.

Yesterday I found the letters about my mother, a little
bundle of them, written at the time of her death. Among
them a letter from Anne Thorp, blessed Anne, who wrote,
"In the dear letter your mother wrote she spoke with joy
of the imaginative and wonderful sharing of living and
dying that you and she had had together."

It is good that I know that now. But I believe that
things happen when the time is ripe and perhaps it is right
that I was given yesterday that balm, and not before.
Failure cannot be erased. It is built in to a life and helps
us grow. Failure cannot be erased, but it can be understood. I think today that Mother *understood*, and that has
made all the difference.

Monday, August 6th

I WOKE AT SIX, opened my eyes, and saw a great orange
and carmine conflagration in the sky, the first sunrise in
three weeks, the first clear air in three weeks. It is cool
and bright at last, and when I came up to my study now
I heard wind stirring the leaves, that watery sound as
cooling as rain. Now I can hardly wait to get out into the

garden and engage in the immense task of weeding out the jungle in the border below the terrace. It has been impossible because of the mosquitoes in the muggy heat we have been in lately.

In spite of all the doors opening these days that permit homosexuals to enter the stream of life instead of being treated as outcasts forever relegated to the backwaters, pariahs whom it is best to pretend do not exist, there is still much civilizing to be accomplished. On the whole, society itself still reacts to certain words with outrage. "Nice people" quiver before the use of certain words; these words are so charged that they create the kind of violent reaction the word "money" roused in my father. His face became red if money had to be discussed and he appeared to be suffering a kind of emotional seizure which made rational discussion impossible. "Lesbian" is such a word today.

These reflections stem from a footnote in Adrienne Rich's new prose book, *On Lies, Secrets and Silence.* In one of the essays she says,

> And I believe it is the Lesbian in every woman who is compelled by female energy, who gravitates toward strong women, who seeks a literature that will express that energy and strength. It is the Lesbian in us who drives us to feel imaginatively, render in language, grasp, the full connection between woman and woman. It is the Lesbian in us who is creative, for the dutiful daughter of fathers in us is only a hack.

At the end of this essay there is a long footnote in which Adrienne Rich tells us of the violent reaction this paragraph caused in her audience of women, and the argument that ensued. Rich goes on to say,

I believe that I failed, in preparing my remarks, to allow for the intense charge of the word *Lesbian,* and for all its deliquescences of meaning from 'man-hater' and 'pervert' to the concepts I was trying to invoke, of the self-chosen woman, the forbidden 'primary intensity' between women, and also the woman who refuses to obey, who has said 'no' to the fathers . . . This experience made me more conscious than ever before of the degree to which, even for Lesbians, the word *Lesbian* has many resonances. Some of us would destroy the word altogether. Others would transform it, still others eagerly speak and claim it after years of being unable to utter it.

Virginia Woolf preferred the word "Sapphist"—possibly because the connotations of Lesbian appear to be chiefly sexual and that is what makes the word frightening. Most people carry around a load of feeling that they bury or pretend is not there because it is too painful and alarming to cope with or because it involves unbearable guilt. Anger against a parent, for example. How much more terrifying than that is being passionately drawn to a member of the same sex!

"They say certain subterranean rivers flow with more force than Niagara" a woman wrote me the other day in another context, but I see this truth constantly in the daily mail. Perhaps two or three times a week I get a letter from an "ordinary woman," not eccentric, not flamboyant, a hard-working mother of a family, sometimes young, more often middle-aged, who has been suffering an earthquake in her private life because she has fallen in love with a woman. There is no thought of divorce . . . these are responsible women who feel committed to stand by husband and children till the end. But they have been starved for mature understanding, for tenderness, for communion. Who could call this "evil"? It is powerfully human, but it imposes a very heavy burden of guilt in our present ethos. Not so much the guilt of infidelity (though that is there, of course) as the guilt of "strangeness," of being in some way abnormal, queer, beyond the pale. To these women I am glad to say, my work has been and is of comfort. They see me perhaps as an acceptable, dignified old woman who can accept the love of women as the creative spur for herself and who has written openly about it. But they know me also, through the work, as a great lover of family life. I am not threatening. I hope I am not.

Tuesday, August 7th

I DID GET TO THE JUNGLE below the terrace yesterday afternoon and had a happy orgy tearing out mint (that great traveller), grass, plantain, dandelions, sorrel, nettles —the names make a delightful litany—and freeing the perennials. I breathe more easily myself as a result. These are joyful days because of the lift in the weather. I was glad of the warmth of Bramble and Tamas last night and lay awake a long time in the moonlight, full moon that drenched the room in its cool brightness. Now again today what pleasure to see the horizon, and a really blue sea, no haze to obscure and deaden everything.

I lay awake a long time thinking about what I wrote yesterday. Doesn't it all come down to trusting feeling?

To trusting one's own self, whatever the world may say or believe? It is hard to go against the ethos, impossible for instance if one were Japanese. For the Japanese ethos substitutes shame for guilt, and shame has to do with the wrong thing as others see it. In the middle of the night I got up and found Ruth Benedict's book about the Japanese *The Chrysanthemum and the Sword* and read what she has to say about shame and guilt.

> The primacy of shame in Japanese life means, as it does in any tribe or nation where shame is deeply felt, that any man watches the judgment of the public upon his deeds. He need only fantasy what the verdict will be, but he orients himself toward the verdict of others.

The danger at present is that shame is coming to dominate when it comes to feeling things which are outside the ethos. I do not believe that women who love women feel guilt, not if it is a true love, but what they do feel is shame, "What would my children think? Or my neighbors?" As I see it, it is shame not guilt that creates the conflict.

If there is very little left in a marriage after twenty years but the sharing of responsibility for the family's life, if there is no sharing of inward life, and very little love, if resentments on both sides have piled up, if there is no give and take, can one speak of infidelity if one of the partners goes outside the marriage for comfort and sustaining love? To what in the end are we faithful? To what must we be faithful? Not surely to the idea of fidelity which precludes growth and change!

It is harder than it looks to be true to one's self. Half the people I see around me have failed in that. They have compromised for the sake of avoiding pain. Or for lack of courage. Or to protect someone they have ceased to love out of a sense of duty. Dutiful women are rarely life givers, even to their children. If a woman is unhappy and embittered and closes the door on her deepest impulse whatever it may be, to write a book, to share love with someone, male or female, outside the marriage, to go on a journey on her own, inward or outward, she is depriving the children of something precious, and they will end by feeling guilty themselves, as though they were taking something from her. Who wants an unhappy embittered mother who makes it clear that she cooks and makes beds not for joy but only out of a sense of duty, and that she feels cramped and cheated of her life as a result?

Thursday, August 9th

YESTERDAY I made my first real sortie since the operation, proof that I am all well. I drove to Wellesley for the day to celebrate Eleanor Blair's eighty-fifth birthday and Marguerite Hearsey's eighty-seventh. My chief anxiety was that the chocolate cake, though covered up in a space blanket with an ice bag, would melt away. It didn't, partly because I had the air conditioner on. It was a sweltering day, but what a pleasure to walk into Eleanor's dear house, and find her blooming, excited because she has made over the top floor into an apartment and has found excellent tenants. On her birthdays (we have shared a good many over the years) she always reminds me of one at Channing Place. As we came down from my study, my mother was standing at the foot of the stairs holding a bunch of flowers from the garden and singing Happy Birthday.

Mother had not known it was a birthday until Eleanor arrived and had dashed out to her garden while we were upstairs to "plunder" as she used to say. The inexhaustible rising to an occasion, the merriment in her eyes, the grace with which she gave—Eleanor remembered it all. I don't see people very often these days who knew my mother, so it was a precious moment.

I never see Eleanor without coming away lifted up by her courage, her inventiveness about the little things in life, and her large vision of what it is all about. And when I left her I had a lively three-quarters of an hour with Marguerite Hearsey and Keats Whiting. As always when I am with these two, we covered the universe, or so it always seems, from Virginia Woolf's ambiguous relation to Katharine Mansfield, to Jimmy Carter and his problems, to my experience in the hospital, to the Sitwell biography which Keats put into my hands as I left. Such eager exchange of all that interests us, and almost everything interests us!

There is also a peculiar pleasure for me in being for once with dear friends older than I am. It sets everything in proportion again and gives me hope. How marvelous to be old and to give courage to those younger than one-self!

Friday, August 10th

IT IS RAINING, a steady gentle rain, hypnotic. And how welcome! Yesterday afternoon I realized that some of the annuals were looking weak like people about to faint and of course I put on the sprinkler at once, but then I realized the whole garden was parched after a week of cool bright air and full sunlight. So this rain is a blessing and will green over the lawn, I hope. Everything looks trim and orderly again, since the men came to prune, as they do each summer due to Mary-Leigh's kindness in keeping the place looking as it should.

What a difference it makes when the French lilac against the outer terrace wall is clipped to make a neat round shape again, and when the wisteria, that creeping menace, is cut back from the porches and the roofs! They took two big branches off the great oak and that means more sun for the annual garden. I might be able to make a place there now for an assortment of day lilies . . . Beverly Hallam's big border of them has been such a success, and the few I have keep flowers in the house in this in-between season for perennials.

Yesterday I saw the doctor, who was delighted with my state and confirmed that I am doing very well indeed. It is more than recovery from an operation. It is due also to consecutive time at home, time to think and to work without extreme pressure at my desk. I begin to feel centered, and, deep down inside, more confident, more my *self* than I have been for two years. I truly believe that the operation acted as a purge, and that the spurt of energy I needed to recover from that has spilled over into psychic energy. I have the wild hope that by the end of the summer I may begin to make notes for a new novel. The journal has proved beneficial in one way, that here I am able to think and speak about women honestly. It is hard to do. I sometimes sit here and think for an hour before I can bring myself to say certain difficult things, difficult because they are not things most people want to hear. But the big block between me and a new novel has been the pressure to do that in fiction. If I can do it here, maybe the door will open again into the novelist's way of creating.

There are novelists who write to a subject, to persuade or proselytize, and I think the trouble with the novella I have laid aside was that it was written to prove something, to attack an ethos, for that is not my gift. It's not what I mean. The only one of my novels written to a thesis, *Crucial Conversations,* is my least favorite, because it is too one-pointed. In the end as a novelist I have wanted to communicate a vision of life, to project my own ethos, not beat down someone else's.

Monday, August 13th

AUGUST ALWAYS IS THE MONTH of "happenings," people turning up on their way Downeast, someone every day now for a while and I feel a little hurried. But what a happy surprise when Alexander Scourby called last night and asked me to lunch tomorrow. He was a member of my company, the Apprentice Theatre, when we played ten modern European plays in rehearsal performance at the New School for Social Research forty-five years ago—not possible! I have heard his beautiful grave voice as the speaker for many documentary films over the years.

On Friday Phil Palmer came for our annual talk. I was rather surprised, and at first a little dismayed, because he brought another Methodist minister with him and I had not expected that. We had a grand talk about everything under the sun as Phil and I always do, and then at the end I discovered why he had brought his friend. They came to ask whether I could come to their annual pastors' assembly next August and be one of three speakers over a period of four days at Center Harbor on Lake Winnepesaukie. "To talk about what?" I asked, touched that they would trust me, would want me (of all people!). But the fact is that ministers, pastors, and priests are often way ahead of their congregations in understanding—more liberal, I suppose I mean to say, deeply concerned about what troubles the mind these days, about the ethos in which we live. The theme next year is to be "healing." What they want of me is to speak, I gathered, about self-renewal, self-healing, and they added, as we spoke, "to speak about vulnerability." The hardest thing for men in the professional classes is to admit to vulnerability as human beings, but when they can their power to communicate is enhanced. "True power is given to the vulnerable."

I believe that, and I was so happy to hear that they believe it too. It comes down to something quite simple: when we admit our vulnerability, we include others; if we deny it, we shut them out. One of the most moving things about Jesus was his extreme vulnerability at the end. He not only taught people, but he became human, and so opened himself to self-doubt and despair. At that point "My God, my God, why hast thou forsaken me?" he conquered the world. Is there any other religious leader who has confessed to such vulnerability? And so whose compassionate understanding is *palpable?*

It was a wonderful blessing to talk with these two men, devoted to such a difficult task, and at the same time learned and open. And for me, of course, wonderful to be *used.*

Tuesday, August 21st

I HAVE BEEN AWAY having a delicious taste of New Hampshire mountains and brooks with Huldah at Center Sandwich, and now I am home again the August pile-up has me in its grip and it is hard to settle down to cogitation. I feel rather like a bewildered old horse trying to sort everything out that must be done, and to "compose the mind," as Marynia Farnham used to say. Mine is a vast formless clutter of impressions and feelings which has its factual counterpart on my desk, letters and papers stacked up in disorder on each side of the typewriter as I type. The effect is of a great deal of noise, a clamor of voices and needs that drown out the gentle sigh of the ocean, and suddenly I remember Marie Gaspar, Jean Dominique's friend, my old teacher who used to say "Balayez-moi tout cela!" (Sweep all that away) when she got impatient. But how is one to do that when human lives are involved?

Yesterday afternoon I did go out for a fine wrestle with
damp earth to transplant the dahlias I grew from seed and
which have done very well indeed this year. They have
so many buds they are not much good for bunches in the
house, so I decided to transplant them into the front border of the terrace where they will make a good show.
Then I did some pulling out of blackberry that is taking
over another part of the garden, but that heavy tugging
with both arms is still a little beyond me, so after filling the
wheelbarrow once, I gave up and came in. It felt good to
be gardening again.

Catherine Becker and her husband, David, and two
teen-age daughters have rented the Firth cottage right
next door for two weeks, and C. and D. came over for a
drink on Sunday, Catherine bearing a piece of apple pie
for my supper and the water color she made two years ago
of the view through French doors in the closed-in porch
where I live when I am downstairs alone. It has a little of
the quality of a Vuillard (the interior that haunts because
it sums up a life or a way of life) and I am awfully happy
to have it. At least for a while it has replaced the Litvak
crayon of a lake in New Jersey over the mantel in the cosy
room.

It was cool enough to have a fire in the library and we
settled in at once to a wholly satisfying talk. I had not
known David, grave, discreet, and bearded, and it was
good to talk about his work a little; he is a print maker,
etchings, unusual in that he makes only one complex work
a year, and when he showed me a reproduction of one I
could see why. It is in itself a whole private mythology
called *Monuments*. Catherine has become a beauty since
I last saw her, as though some inward tussle to become her
real self had brought her out in her full womanly strength.
What staggered me with joy was the perfect openness of

these two, how we began at once to talk about real things
. . . it is always so with the artists who come here. I am at
home in my real world with them, and we exchange our
fears and conflicts because we know that we share the
same ones. Every artist lives in a constant state of self-
criticism, self-doubt, and in near despair a good deal of the
time. David, for instance, is being pushed by his dealer to
produce more, but one does not produce a meditation in
a trice, and the very quality of his work precludes "production" at a fast pace. Catherine is torn between poetry
and painting and at the moment is stymied in each direc-
tion. How dear it was to feel her appreciation of him,
"David is rare, a rare person" she said, and she also said
that she had learned in the two years since we last met to
see him objectively, to see him *in himself* as himself. This
has come about through a lot of pain on each side. David
said, "Catherine is an extraordinary woman."

To see a person for himself or herself, not for one's
feelings about them, requires wisdom, and I must assume
that it is part of the ascension of true love beyond the
initial passion and need. On the way there are frightful
resentments and irritations caused by intrinsic differences
of temperament and many a marriage or love affair bogs
down as a result. How does one achieve perfect detachment? Partly perhaps by accepting the essence of a being
for what it is, not wishing to change it, accepting.

I wish I were as wise as they, these two artists, these
friends.

Friday, August 24th

THE DAY BEFORE YESTERDAY I went down to Cambridge
and stopped on the way to see Judy in her new "home."
Her windows look out on trees and the atmosphere is
sunny and peaceful. The move has been a wise one. She
did not recognize me, "babbles of green fields," and I shall
leave it there.

Feeling bereft and shaken I went to have lunch with
Connie, Judy's sister, and Trish, her niece. Judy's family
treat me as family and I flew into Connie's little house like
a bird into a nest, grateful for a haven at that moment.
Connie does everything with exquisite taste; the chicken
salad made with a little cut up grapes and apple was delicious. Wild-blueberry muffins, too. It occurs to me that
someone should write a cookbook for the stricken!

From there I went to Cora DuBois in Cambridge to
have a rest before meeting Carol Heilbrun for dinner in
the Square. Cora and Jeanne Taylor are also people who
create havens, and Cora and I had a good talk out in the
garden with Silas, their tiger cat, sitting, paws tucked in,
on the terrace wall, blinking his wide green eyes at us.
Cora, like me, is recovering from surgery and pleased me
very much by asking to see my scar. No one else has done
so. Next morning we exchanged "views" in a nice compet-
itive way like two small boys.

These two visits have sent me back to my poem "Of

Havens." It was written as an answer to the hippies, an
attempt to suggest that maintaining a home is not to be
despised, and is as much a gift to those strangers who
come into it as to the family inside. This is part of it—

> Though we dream of never having a wall against
> All that must flow and pass, and cannot be caught,
> An ever-welcoming self that is not fenced,
> Yet we are tethered still to another thought:
> The unsheltered cannot shelter, the exposed
> Exposes others; the wide open door
> Means nothing if it cannot be closed.

> Those who create real havens are not free.
> Hold fast, maintain, are rooted, dig deep wells;
> Whatever haven human love may be,
> There is no freedom without sheltering walls.
> And when we imagine wings that come and go
> What we see is a house, and a wide-open window.

It was a huge pleasure to be in leafy Cambridge, which
I have always loved best in summer, remembering the
teas in the garden at Channing Place, and Judy's and my
evening walks along old brick-paved sidewalks under the
elms and maples, looking up at lighted windows high up
under the eaves where someone must be studying. Despite all the changes Cambridge still has great charm. It
is invigorating to see so many faces of character walking
along any street, young and old, purposeful people one
senses. And it was an added pleasure to walk with Carol
to Ferdinand's for dinner through the Radcliffe quadran-
gle where I once tried to teach a class under a flowering
apple tree, and learned that teaching out of doors on a
May day is just not possible. Who can listen to words when
there are bees in the apple blossoms buzzing away? And

lovers, passing by, arm in arm, and chequered light on an open book? No one in his senses can, and students are quite right to wish to study only spring.

Carol Heilbrun and I rarely meet, but when we do it is always a festival of exchanges about our very different lives yet containing so many explosively natural points of contact that the deep union where values are concerned leaves me feeling nourished, and also hungry for more. We do not talk about literature, or only glancingly, which is odd. I never leave her without feeling immense joy and gratitude that she has agreed to be my literary executor . . . how lucky I am that a woman so rich in gifts and responsibilities to her own family and her own work and her own students, would take on such a task in my behalf!

There is no other friend with whom I laugh as much, as delightedly, the laughter of recognition, and often the recognition of how hard and even impossible life can be. Carol, too, is recovering from an unwarrantedly cruel attack in the Sunday *Times* some months ago. We had not met since then, and I suppose in a way we did what Cora and I did, showed each other our scars and laughed together at what hurt so much and has been overcome.

Carol has come to the conclusion that real literature today must survive outside the media, and does so by means of a network of readers of sensitivity and good will who share their discoveries. I heartily agree.

It is very easy to laugh when one feels that pain or an ordeal has been completely understood; and it is impossible to laugh when one feels that it has not been understood. It is then that anger takes over. And also self-pity, I am afraid.

Saturday, August 25th

DORIS GRUMBACH is here for two nights and a day and it is good to know someone is working downstairs, a fellow writer. It is rarely that a writer comes to stay, and it makes me see once more that no one who is not engaged in this particular struggle, to bring a vision of life out into words, can really understand what it is all about and the hazards that assail the writer every day of his life, not least that a great success like hers with *Chamber Music* terrifies: what if one cannot do it again? It is wonderful to be able to talk freely without being thought absurd, self-pitying, or narcissistic about these silent battles. Very often it is not necessary to finish a sentence the laughter of recognition is so immediate. It is a feast for me to have seen Carol so recently and now Doris, each a writer whom I admire and with whom I can share.

It is a long while since I have come upon a book that nourishes places in my inner being that have been starved for faith and renewal. Every day we face such disasters, such horrors, in the newspapers. We are all overwhelmed by tragedies about which we can do very little; it finally becomes like a mountain of dirt and despair, stifling. Where to look for hope in mankind itself? So I am devouring Philip Hallie's *Lest Innocent Blood Be Shed*. It is about Hallie's discovery one day during his perusal of documents on the holocaust of the story of a Protestant village in Southern France which had risked destruction by protecting and hiding Jews. The story struck him like a blow, and he found himself weeping. As he describes it

> I reached up to my cheek to wipe away a bit of dust, and I felt tears upon my fingertips. Not one or two drops; my whole cheek was wet.
>
> 'Oh,' my sentinel mind told me, 'you are losing your grasp on things again. Instead of learning about cruelty, you are becoming one more of its victims. You are doing it again.' I was disgusted with myself for daring to intrude.
>
> And so I closed the book and left my college office. When I came home, my Italian wife and my turbulent children, as they have never failed to do, distracted me noisily. I hardly felt the spear that had gone through me. But that night when I lay on my back in bed with my eyes closed, I saw more clearly than ever the images that had made me weep. I saw the two clumsy buses of the Vichy French police pull into the village square. I saw the police captain facing the pastor of the village and warning him that if he did not give up the names of the Jews they had been sheltering in the village, he and his fellow pastor as well as the families who had been caring for the Jews, would be arrested. I saw the pastor refuse to give up these people who had been strangers in his village, even at the risk of his own destruction.
>
> Then I saw the only Jew the police could find, sitting in an otherwise empty bus. I saw a thirteen-year-old boy, the son of the pastor, pass a piece of his precious chocolate through the window to the prisoner, while twenty gendarmes who were guarding the lone prisoner watched. And then I saw the villagers passing their little gifts through the window until there were gifts all around him—most of them food in those hungry days during the German occupation of France.

Lying there in bed, I began to weep again. I thought, 'Why run away from what is excellent simply because it goes through you like a spear?' Lying there, I knew that always a certain region of my mind contained an awareness of men and women in bloody white coats breaking the bones of six- or seven- or eight-year-old Jewish children in order, the Nazis said, to study the processes of natural healing in young bodies. All of this I knew. But why not know joy? Why not leave root room for comfort? . . .

To the dismay of my wife, I left the bed unable to say a word, dressed, crossed the dark campus on a starless night, and read again those few pages on the village of Chamon-sur-Lignon. And to my surprise, again the spear, again the tears, again the frantic painful pleasure that spills into the mind when a deep, deep need is being satisfied, or when a deep wound is starting to heal.

And so Hallie decided to go to the village and to talk with the people there who might still be alive and remember. The book is about his search and what he found. What it tells us in essence is once more that one person, in this case the pastor André Trocmé, can still restore to the world compassion and the belief in the preciousness of every human life. He can do it alone against all the odds. Hallie says, "I needed this understanding in order to redeem myself—and possibly others—from the coercion of despair."

Over and over again we have to push aside the mountains of bad news, the mountainous sufferings of which we are reluctant witnesses and single out a single human being, always go back to the individual man, to the caring ones. They are and always have been a network and they represent the communion of saints on earth. What they do is to wrench us out of despairing passivity, *anomie,* and bring us back into an ethical universe, as Trocmé himself had done for a whole village.

Monday, August 27th

I LOVE MONDAYS, the tide rising again after the lull of the weekend. Doris left after breakfast yesterday and a young woman from California turned up (I had forgotten she was to call me) to take me out to lunch. I had hoped for one clear day to pull myself together, but as sometimes happens, her visit was to the point and made me think about energy and how it can be renewed when one is tired. Jan has a full-time job as a librarian and writes poems, and she spoke of being tired a lot of the time, as who would not with a nine-to-five job, and a demanding avocation?

The problem is perhaps to learn how to come to a full stop. I am lucky enough to be able to do this by lying down for an hour in the afternoon, my way of making a shift from one kind of work to another. But someone with a full-time job can't take that way, and now and then I am too on edge, too dispersed by visits and the pile-up on my desk, to let go. That happened the other day, so I got up and went out into the garden to pull weeds for an hour and it was wonderful to feel the whole nervous system quieting down. When I am gardening I do not think of anything at all; I am wholly involved in the physical work and when I go in, I feel whole again, centered. Why? I

think maybe it is because when things pile up one does nothing with the whole of oneself. The next thing on the calendar is already moving in before one has finished whatever it is one is at. Then pressure builds up. Gardening empties the mind. Music can do it. Ten minutes of "giving all the action up" can do it. And for me, reading a single poem sometimes can do it. The knots in the mind unravel. The thick air clears. I find composure again.

We are such intricate machines and treat the machine badly because we expect too much of ourselves. Machines, even complex machines, do one thing at a time, and the answer to fatigue may often be to settle for that. The constant remaking of order out of chaos is what life is all about, even in the simplest domestic chores such as clearing the table and washing the dishes after a meal. No one fails to wish to do that and to do it, but when it comes to the inner world, the world of feeling and thinking, many people leave the dishes unwashed for weeks so no wonder they feel ill and exhausted. The deeper the experience, the more time is required to sort it out. One of the great values of passionate love is that the very force of it eliminates clutter—the non-essential falls away; non-essential anxieties fall away. We are as naked and open as small children, and they, of course, have much to teach us about total concentration.

The autumn is coming. The crickets sing their autumn song. I saw red leaves on the path when I walked Tamas yesterday. The woods are full of mushrooms now, like baroque, somewhat sinister flowers. I saw a woodcock for the first time in years. It always seems an incredible bird and makes me laugh with pleasure at the long perpendicular beak and small flat eyes, and the no-tail. Absurd, delightful creature. The real event of that day.

Tuesday, August 28th

I HAD CATHERINE AND DAVID BECKER over for supper last
night, a celebration (though I had not known that) of their
seventeenth wedding anniversary and of my finally send-
ing the new book of poems off in the morning. We were
all three in a cheerful state of mind, having drinks in the
cosy room, waiting for the lobster water to boil, when the
light darkened in an ominous way and suddenly we were
in the center of a tremendous and terrifying thunderstorm. I ran around closing windows against sheets of rain
and wild moments of white glare before another clap of
thunder, while Catherine called Bramble whom she had
seen streak past the windows. But Bramble had taken
refuge under the bushes on the terrace and would not
come out.

  Then we were suddenly in total darkness—luckily not
until the lobsters were in and nearly cooked! I found candles and a battery-run camp light for the kitchen, and we
settled in for another drink. How beautiful the room
looked by candlelight, the two candles in silver candles-
ticks Judy and I always used on Christmas Eve. Last night
they illuminated a stem of white lilies, their heraldic form,
and the dark red stamens, and we looked at them together in silent admiration. This soft warm light on petals
made electric light seem hard and soulless, and it was fun
to be together and to go on talking of the state of the
world while the storm raged on outside. Bramble finally

came in, wet and furious, while Tamas snoozed. He is, curiously enough, not afraid of thunderstorms, and keeps his composure better than I do . . . so it is he who comforts me when we are alone in one.

This morning I am tired. I couldn't believe the power was still off when I woke at six and went down to the unwashed dishes to heat water on the sterno, and take coffee and cold cereal up to my bed for breakfast. For once I longed to stay there and sleep, as Bramble was doing on the end of the bed. But then the lights came on and I felt the tug of my desk, and all that has to be done on a day between visits. Blue Jenkins, an old friend from Nelson days, comes tomorrow for two nights.

Saturday, September 1st

AFTER THE HUMID HEAT it was amazing yesterday to wake to clear air. It is still with us, a silent shining day with only the chug of a lobster boat in the distance to break the silence. It is an inner silence as well as an outer one because the Beckers left this morning from the cottage next door and I took Blue to the bus in Portsmouth yesterday morning.

I'm sad that the one day Blue was here was hot and depressing, but we did have a short walk on Long Sands Beach, among some solemn gulls, a flight of sandpipers skimming over the waves, and—amazingly enough—very few people considering that it was still August. But of course what we both needed was to catch up and have good hours of quiet talk, so the weather did not spoil our exchange of lives. I haven't seen Blue for three years and she is now a grandmother.

That afternoon I got ready to say goodbye to Catherine Becker, who was due at four-thirty, by lying out on the terrace for a half hour. Why do I do this so rarely? It was cool and bright, the hour when the birds begin to fly over on their evening errands. I drank the silence like a magic liquor, thinking how lucky I am to live where it is often absolutely still, feeling the silence literally "fall" and all the agitations and pleasures of this very full week quiet down like silt in the bottom of a glass.

After a while I began to think about how precarious life is for all of us these days. I often have the sensation of falling, often in the night I have it when I wake and can't go to sleep again, the sensation that everything we once thought of as steadfast, dependable, always-to-be-there has begun to fall away and that we, inevitably, are falling away with it—the earth itself being depleted, and the ocean, and all the fish and mammals therein slowly being snuffed out. The *New Yorker* has an article this week on Kew Gardens and endangered plants which are far more numerous even than endangered animals, I learned.

When one then contemplates man himself and his destructive ways (Mountbatten and his grandson blown up by an IRA bomb, the boat people floating into our consciousness with their desperate cries for help, "and more" as they say in the TV ads) it is clear that hope is a very scarce commodity these days. It takes courage to stop "doing" and start "thinking" and many people cannot face at all the emptiness, loss of the faith that anything good and constructive is still possible.

Then I remembered Jean Dominique and how often she quoted Péguy who in the darkest hours of World War

I could speak of "la petite Espérance" who in spite of everything accompanies each of us and tells us to be patient and never to give up.

Sunday, September 2nd

YESTERDAY AFTERNOON I did a big piece of gardening, trying to clean up the iris bed which is a thick mass of weeds, the plants themselves buried alive and strangled. It is a job I usually do in June, but of course this year I couldn't. Raymond came and worked at pulling out blackberry from under the pines—it has almost taken over the ground cover there and was even catching in and tearing the tuberous begonia petals. The savagery of weeds! But I had to stop after an hour and again lay down on the terrace to taste the rare clear air, the blue sea and the intermittent punctuating sails but it was not like yesterday's nourishing silence because I failed to become a good instrument for it.

I knew the tide of woe was rising, that woe that seizes me like anger and is a form of anger, and I didn't know what to do to stop it, so I got up and picked flowers, cooked my dinner, looked at the news, all the same usual routine that can often ward off the devils or suddenly clear the air as when a thunderstorm seems to be coming and then dissipates. It is the first time I have been overcome in this way since the operation and I had hoped it would never happen again. Why did it?

I think it always happens when there is a galaxy of

problems that get knit together into one huge outcry
against the sense of being abandoned, of orphanhood
. . . and perhaps then over-giving as a way of handling it.
The week has been too full. There has been too much
experience and too little time to sort it out, too little time
between one thing and another. Then on Saturday when
I least expected it a blow from the fates. Some months ago
when I was anxious about the hospital bills, I had asked
Norton & Co. to give me an estimate on what the bi-
yearly royalties would be in September. They gave me a
rough estimate of $13,000. The check yesterday was for
under $9,000. I had counted on the extra, have ordered
new curtains for my bedroom (the old ones are in tatters)
and felt just the small margin necessary for one to feel
"more abundant life." When the check came for so much
less I felt constricted, no longer able to breathe that freer
air. It came a week after Doris was here telling me of all
the luck, deserved luck, that *Chamber Music* has had, the
last item, $70,000 for movie rights. I rejoice for her, but
it does rub it in that I still, after thirty-two books, make a
precarious living. God knows what the oil bills will be this
winter.

I realize and tell myself often how lucky I am to be
published at all, and to hear from so many people that the
work has been worth the struggle, that it does nourish and
sustain. I am lucky, too, to make my living at it, even such
a precarious living. And I know that without anxiety about
money I might become fat and lazy and stop writing for
publication altogether.

But the woe was not all made of that blow by any
means. One woe opens others. What is the nature of a love
that cannot comfort or sustain, that has made me a whip-
ping boy for the very things that others praise and find

nourishment in? I woke this morning thinking that fire and water cannot mix, air and fire, yes; earth and water, yes. But water puts fire out, and fire troubles water in a non-productive way. That woe is at the center of my life and has been for two years.

And the third woe yesterday that brought on the storm is that over-giving, by that I mean trying to give what is needed to too many people, boomerangs. It is exactly the same reaction as when I have done too many poetry readings and fall into depression as a result. Over-giving cannot be helped but one pays a high price for it.

So I create a fifth woe by pouring all this out into poor Barbara's ear who has, with Ann, been entertaining too much family and is as overtired as I am! The telephone can be a dangerous outlet for a tempest and I used it badly last night.

Monday, September 3rd, Labor Day

HUMID HEAT, RAIN. Now at nearly eleven there is a wide band of light above the horizon and a pale sun through the shifting clouds. I had been fiddling around all morning, unable to get hold of a thread I might follow, and then for a moment looked down at the winding grassy path that goes down to the cliff and the sea. It is most beautiful now when the field grasses are pale gold and frame its meandering line on each side. It has always been for me a magic path. When I first saw it, it seemed something remembered in another life, something I wanted to live with and it weighed heavily in my decision to move here from Nelson—a grassy path going down to the sea.

I see it best from this high window on the third floor where I sit to work. It is a constant companion to my thinking, making me slow down and take it easy, saunter instead of run, because there is time before I reach ocean, the timelessness at the end.

Until now I had felt in a childish way that life was always somewhere ahead preparing surprises, that something amazing was about to happen, and it often did. Now I am coming to understand that my life is over or nearly. The timelessness at the end approaches. It has been a rich life, filled to the brim with work and love, and I am really quite ready to let it go. Maybe this is the Labor Day mood, a dull holiday at best, the end of summer.

Tuesday, September 4th

A THICK AND TERRIBLE NIGHT, so humid that I lay in bed in a sweat and finally turned on the big fan for awhile. I had a nightmare that all the letters I have written this weekend had got lost in someone's pocket. Now the air has cleared. It is a fine still cool morning and I begin to feel the wind in my sails for my trip down to the Cape to see Rene's little house for the first time. Two nights and two days away breaks the thread of the journal as I have learned. On the other hand I shall have hours to think in as I drive down and back, and maybe those few seeds I have sown for a new novel will sprout.

I really long to be immersed again in creating a life or lives quite outside my own. The big question that has to be solved is the form. It could be a huge regular novel about a long life, but my instinct tells me that I must find a way to do this impressionistically, by eliding and condensing to bring a long life vividly to the reader through what might be small vignettes. I suppose I am taking refuge in creation because I am shocked by my childish behavior, lack of control the other night and my unregenerate self, and because I think I know that what makes me a person often hard to live with, and even disgraceful (all those tears and rages) are what makes me a good writer. Absolute control is destructive to the artist always, even in his work. There has to be room for the angels and devils to operate. How to be perfectly open and perfectly controlled? It is simply not possible. So in the end I have to accept myself as a useful creator (at least I can believe that now in my old age) and a difficult human being. And at the same time to honor and love the balanced people whose primary creation is themselves. Then I remember Winifred Wilkinson saying one day "I hate balanced people," and I must confess that I feel a lot better when one of them lets some anger out for a change. It makes them more human. Perfection is cold and has slippery sides, but the human with all its faults is eminently huggable.

Saturday, September 8th

BEFORE LEAVING FOR THE CAPE I decided that a swelling in Tamas's ear must be looked at, and trundled him off to the vet Tuesday afternoon. It turned out to be a blood blister caused by scratching and when I went to fetch him yesterday after the operation Dr. Stevens told me that the ears were infected as well. Anyway I could bring him home, his poor ear stapled with protective material on both sides of it. How empty the place feels when he is not here! It was less than twenty-four hours, as I left for the Cape early Wednesday morning, but his absence tore a huge hole in the fabric of life here. Absence, absence was in the air, and without his comforting body beside me, I slept badly.

He does not come up here to my study, and spends most afternoons in his secret hiding place under the hedge on the terrace, so we are often apart during the day, but I know he is there, hear an occasional bark, and am comforted by his mere presence—presence, which like absence when he was at the vet's, is quite intangible since I feel it in the atmosphere whether he is close by or not.

My life here is to a large extent composed of such silent or hardly audible presences, the ocean for one. When I have been away and come back, it is for a short time as though a frail web, as frail as a spider's web, had been torn and must be re-woven out of air and thought.

I have known Rene Morgan for at least ten years, but had not yet been to see her in the little house in Harwich she built after her retirement. We managed a swim in the ocean, in delicious warm water, my first swim since the operation; and walked along the shore, littered with seaweed still from the storm, listened to records, did some lovely exploring on small roads among the endless variations on the gray shingled Cape salt box, and I was pleased by the horizontal landscape, very few two-storied houses, very few tall trees, and by the salt marshes already turning gold.

But what moved me most was the gathering together in that brief forty-eight hours of what seemed like the harvest of our friendship, and made me think about friendship and how it is built. I had been thinking all the way down about what an unregenerate character I am and whether I shall ever improve at all, so it was a real comfort when Rene said she felt I was far more serene than when she first knew me and used to come to Nelson. Our friendship has grown little by little and has taken a lot of patience on her side, but she has been from the beginning one of the few people who truly want to help me, one of the few who never comes to see me without seeing something that needs doing and doing it. While I was there she was determined to solve one small domestic problem, to find the iron stem for the stone of a Cape Cod lighter for me. We tried half a dozen antique shops and hardware stores in our rambles, but had no luck. But last evening she called me to say she had found the solution and would bring a new stem up when she next visits me here. She has been, over the years, aware of my state of mind, calls often to see if I am all right and is like those intangible presences I spoke of, a steadfast loving presence through all I do and am. That, perhaps, is what friendship is all about. At the root of it is an abiding faith in me as a writer and as a person.

What is the exchange? Why has it been worth it for her? She has listened to my often violent opinions about art, religion, and politics and has not been offended. What can I give her in return? Perhaps she values intimacy with a creator whom she respects, values it enough to take the rough with the smooth, and knows that the rough is inevitable where such tensions are involved. But lately, as she and I each grow older, I have been able now and then to see when she is tired and insist that she have a rest before she leaves here after we have had lunch. Little by little she has come to understand in what deep respect I hold her and her values, and how much I have wanted to share in her anxiety about her sister who has had difficult operations and also heart attacks in these past years, that I have come to be woven into her life as she has woven herself into mine. None of this happens overnight. For friendship exactly like love has to be won, and won over a longer time than passionate love takes to root itself in a life. I felt yesterday that Rene and I are well-rooted in each other's lives and that is a great blessing.

Monday, September 10th

THESE ARE THE GREAT DAYS when clarity comes back to the air and all is a radiant suspense before the first leaf falls. Autumn is on the threshold, but for a week or two we have the best of everything. A still center before the

wheel turns. I long to meet these days with an equal
serenity, but I am troubled and exhausted by the battle
that never stops as I try to understand what has gone
wrong with the major relationship in my life and why
after a year and a half of this I am still on the rack. Obses-
sions such as this get in the way of everything I want to
do, and only when I am out working hard in the garden
do I escape the echoes and reverberations of pain. I have
believed that if I waited and believed and loved as well
as I could, we would find our way out. There are reasons
why we cannot live together on a permanent basis and it
may be that if that is not possible, if two people can never
share daily life—the nourishing and calming routines over
a sustained period of time in every year—*feeling* frays
out. No one can live on wine alone.

Looking over an old journal I came upon something a
friend once said to me about a difficult relationship, "We
do not need a psycho-analyst, we need a referee." It made
me laugh with recognition.

The other night I dreamed that I was some sort of
aquatic plant or low form of animal life, floating on stag-
nant water. I saw it as an image outside myself and saw
that whatever being it was had put down long trailing
tendrils or roots and was floating around trying desperately to find nourishment. I am literally starving for a kind
of caring and sensitivity that appears not to be available,
and because it is not, the whole creative imagination has
been absorbed for months in trying to get food. Nothing
else.

Why then go on? Why not give up? Fidelity to an
imaginary world that I myself have created out of nothing
only because I needed it so much, is not a fidelity worth
having or worth giving. Here perhaps age does play a
part. I am too old to "move on" as I could when I was

young and the choices seemed infinite. I lack the courage
to break away from the little I have and to start falling
through empty space, another terrifying dream that has
repeated itself several times lately.

All this being my present state, anxiety about the new
book of poems, *Halfway to Silence,* a book of love poems,
which is now at Norton, is far worse than it usually is. The
poems were true when they were written and are still
true, but the experience they relate has changed. In this
context I comfort myself at this moment by copying out
parts of a letter that reached me sometime ago and has
stuck with me as few letters do. Virginia Russell says,

Reading a book by the astronomer Jastrow lately has provoked
a train of thought that has kept me good company for days. I
find myself staring out the window with the bed half-made,
pillow in hand, lost 'among the stars' for who knows how long.

If Time exists only when there is matter in motion, say the
physicists, then this Newtonian, Euclidean world of time we
live in is merely Chronos, chronology. But there is also Kairos,
the realm of timelessness (which by definition is still a concept
of time) and Kairos, suspension from time, is, I think, what the
artist or the mystic knows during what we call moments of
inspiration. That is, timelessness is not Time going on and on
(the usual notion of Eternity) but another kind of Time or realm
in which life (of another kind) is sustained.

And one who creates or one who prays perhaps moves over
into that other realm for 'brief visits' and returns in some way
changed. . . .

Maybe the work of an artist lives, not just within the
reader's or the viewer's Chronos-bound thoughts but beyond
time, in Kairos. Maybe thought as a phenomenon belongs to
Kairos. It is true, I think, that the work of art has a life of its own.
This may relate to the fact that it is fertilized, as it were, in a
realm or by something from that realm beyond the artist, beyond the Chronos in which the artist usually exists. In this sense

maybe the artist functions as the womb in which art gestates;
then he/she labors to bring it forth. And it wears his/her genes!
I'm not sure how such an idea accounts for the art that is mon-
strous. Except that there is a Shadow side to things. Or else it
is ersatz, not art.

I reach and have reached the timeless moment, the
pure suspension within time, only through love.

Wednesday, September 12th

I GO OUT SO RARELY in the evening that it was an event
to drive out in the dusk and cross the river to Susan Garrett's last night at sunset. We sat on the large porch of the
Garretts' ancient house and watched as the sun came out
from under clouds and turned the river to gold, a golden
river flowing very fast out to sea on the ebb tide, while a
few cars crossed the bridge and the few boats still left in
the harbor tugged at their moorings. It is much more
human and peopled on the York River than here where
I am. There is intimacy within its distances. That hour
while we drank Scotch and caught up on our lives was
pure magic.

So what I said the day before yesterday about the
timeless moment being associated for me only with passionate love was not quite true. Maybe the timeless moment comes to us when we are centered and so can truly
see. I was thinking about this early this morning as the sun

rose while I read Henri J. M. Nouwen's small book of sermons *Out Of Solitude* and came upon this paragraph,

> Somewhere we know that without a lonely place our lives are in danger. Somewhere we know that without silence words lose their meaning, that without listening speech no longer heals, that without distance closeness cannot cure. Somewhere we know that without a lonely place our actions quickly become empty gestures. The careful balance between silence and words, withdrawal and involvement, distance and closeness, solitude and community forms the basis of the Christian life.

It is so with the artist's life always and finding the balance is the never-ending struggle. It is quite unbalanced of me to spend about eighty percent of my working time answering letters and I am beginning to see that it is not productive, even to the recipients of the letters who in the long run would prefer another book to a hurried response . . . or so I must try to believe.

I am also coming to understand, though with difficulty, that it is perhaps not true that what cannot be expressed does not exist. This is the writer's belief, of course. Words are what he or she lives by, and his whole life is the struggle to express in words what he believes and feels. It is ironic in a no doubt salutary way that I am in love with a person who cannot express love in any way, not by small spontaneous gestures such as a passing kiss, or a brief message flung into the river of time that would reassure, and never never in words.

When I was teaching, one of my bêtes-noires was a phrase like "I cannot describe it," "beyond words," or "I know but I can't say it." My response was always what you cannot say or describe you have not seen or felt. But there is something else involved. Words can be debased by overuse. The too-expressive may in the end lack substance.

Still, a person who cannot express love is stopping the flow of life, is censoring where censorship is a form of self-indulgence, the fear of giving oneself away.

Nouwen goes on in his little book,

> In solitude we can slowly unmask the illusion of our possessiveness and discover in the center of our own self that we are not what we can conquer, but what is given to us. . . . It is in this solitude that we discover that being is more important than having, and that we are worth more than the result of our efforts. In solitude we discover that life is not a possession to be defended, but a gift to be shared. It's there we recognize that the words we speak are not just our own, but are given to us; that the love we can express is part of a greater love; and that the new life we bring forth is not a property to cling to, but a gift to be received.

Many people feel orphaned (we are all sooner or later orphans), and in many cases unfairly punished by life. Like me they search frantically for a mother or a rock for shelter from that falling into emptiness about which I dreamed the other night. But we all finally have to come to see that only when we have learned to mother ourselves and to shelter ourselves are we ready for communion with others on any level, when in fact acute need has ceased to make neurotic demands. Oh, but it is not easy! "Without distance closeness cannot cure."

And all this as a result of a wonderful supper with Susan. We came in from the porch as it got cold for a second drink by the fire in the small cosy library, the black dog asleep on the hearth, and then ate by candlelight. Let us not forget the importance of mere food! We had lamb au jus, a remarkable ratatouille, the best I ever had, with cheese and a grater there to use on it, avocado and crisp Boston lettuce salad, and finally strawberries.

This house was Susan's father's, and is very old. We ate on plates that had belonged to her grandmother. The library is lined on all walls (it has a low ceiling) by books of poems and on poetry. (George Garrett is a poet as well as a novelist.) When I think of Susan I think of instant response . . . the way we plunge into the real things even when we have met for a moment in the store. It is no joke to be married to a writer even such a genial, witty, and generous one as George is, for any woman married to a writer has to bear the burden of immense never-ending insecurities, anguish about the present work, despair at bad reviews or neglect, to be the ever-present comforter and believer. Susan and George have three college-age children, so she has mothered four people over the years, and now she is the very efficient mother of a hospital. The word that comes to mind about this remarkable person is "seasoned." And there she is, open and lovable and vulnerable as a child, and at the same time strong, giving, mature in her ability to detach herself and see things with wry humor. We do not see each other often but I think of her as one of the treasures life has given me. So much reverberates after we part.

Thursday, September 13th

IT IS A VERY LONG TIME since I have felt so charged with psychic energy, so alive and on the brink of creation . . . in fact in the last three days I have written two poems. I cannot rest, and get up from my usual nap in a half hour, unable to "let down." It is partly the autumn weather, the clarity of the air, and the upward curve that autumn has always meant for me, since I was a child and it meant going back to school to which I looked forward immensely. But I feel sure that it is chiefly because I am letting go, beginning to realize inside myself, not only think about, the necessity for distancing myself from a love that has proved too destructive. For months I simply could not admit that it had to end, the pain seemed too excruciating to face. Now I begin to live into the reality, that my true self has been nearly obliterated in the long struggle to understand. Let the obsession go, and I shall be free to create (there has been a censor in my mind) and become a good friend. I can cast out the wrong idea of fidelity and understand that in the end one cannot be faithful in the true life-giving sense if it means being unfaithful to oneself.

On Tuesday the *Times* had a piece on Medal Day at the MacDowell Colony. John Cheever is the recipient this year and I was pleased by what he is quoted as saying in his speech of acceptance. "There is always the possibility that as one grows old, one won't be able to write," he remarked. And later on, "But writers have very little to say about continuing to write. I did wake one morning and think 'Ah, but I don't *have* to write another novel.' And then I realized I had no choice. The need to write comes from the need to make sense of one's life and discover one's usefulness. For me, it is the most intimate form of communicating about love and memory and nostalgia. As close as I am to my son, there are still things I can't say to him that I can say in fiction. I feel on this particular afternoon or in this particular light that to write is a sort of giftedness."

What hit me most in this was the combination of "make sense of one's life" and "discover one's usefulness." For one can't do one without the other. And to some extent if one is a writer one comes to make sense of one's life by saying where one is. Every one of my novels has been an attempt to do this, and of course the journals are exactly that in a far easier and less exacting form. The novels, if I think in musical terms, are the symphonies and the journals are the sonatas. The poems then are songs.

I had lunch with Heidi yesterday, our weekly lunch that is one of the few ceremonies of my life here that has anything to do with people, so it is precious and sustaining in a very special way. When I got home I couldn't rest, so made a stew so there will be something to eat for a few days. Then I went out into the garden to finish weeding the iris bed. It is satisfying to pull out the long white roots of the witch grass, and to clear space around the iris roots. I got so happily absorbed that I forgot the simmering stew and it burned, not beyond salvage, but I was furious with myself. Never mind, I would rather have iris to pick next summer than stew today!

Tamas waits for me to get up every afternoon and if I rest too long barks to tell me it is time for gardening. He comes and lies down beside me while I work, and Bramble often makes an appearance at that time, winds herself around me with loud purrs and then runs away on her autumn errands which are chiefly catching mice in the newly mown field.

The raspberries, the late ones, are ripening and if the wasps don't eat them all, there should be some for Huldah when she comes in early October, for she loves them.

Thinking about the garden calms me. I have felt like a firecracker about to go off.

Saturday, September 15th

THE END OF HURRICANE FREDERICK that did so much damage in Mobile came to us as a swirl of tropical air and gusts of warm rain yesterday. Today all is washed clean, the ocean dark autumn blue for the first time, and I feel at peace. Perhaps Heidi and I can sit out on the terrace this afternoon when she comes to bring me some corn from her garden.

Nouwen speaks of care in the little book I have been reading a page at a time. He says, "The word 'care' finds its roots in the Gothic 'Kara' which means lament. The basic meaning of care is: to grieve, to experience sorrow, to cry out with." And later on,

The friend who cares makes it clear that whatever happens in the external world, *being present to each*

other is what really matters. In fact, it matters more
than pain, illness, or even death. It is remarkable how
much consolation and hope we can receive from authors who, while offering no answers to life's questions, have the courage to articulate the situation of
their lives in all honesty and directness. Kierkegaard,
Sartre, Camus, Hammarskjöld, and Merton—none of
them have offered solutions. Yet many of us who
have read their works have found new strength to
pursue our own search. Their courage to enter so
deeply into human suffering and *to become present
to their own pain* gave them the power to speak
healing words. (*Underlining* mine.)

I have been carrying this around in my mind, and
thinking about caring, and at the same time trying to
"become present to my own pain," as a result of a letter
from a friend in England that accuses me of betraying
human dignity because I have written not only of Judy's
loss of her mental powers but also her loss of physical
control, that I have talked so openly of what senility
means. My friend believes that that is a betrayal of all that
Judy was, and is "offensive." Many people would agree
with this. It is comforting to know that Judy's own family
has not been among them.

Why then have I done it? I begin to wonder myself. I
think it is partly because I have wanted to be present to
the pain of those who, like me, have had to witness the
obliteration of all that a person they have loved deeply
really was, through this inadmissable deterioration. Judy
is not Judy now. It is not the senile person who suffers, but
those who have to witness and be present at the disinte-
gration of a human being. No one who has not experienced this can imagine, perhaps, how agonizing it can

be. For a time there are moments of recognition, remembrance, and communion. They make all the nursing and physical care worth it. But the time comes when there are no longer any such moments, when one cannot find anything of the "real person" with which one can still communicate on any level. An irritable, totally selfish infant has replaced the wise, dignified, loving person one loved, *and still loves,* and that is why the pain is so acute. When someone dies, the person transcends his or her death. In some ways we are more with them, more in touch, than ever before. The essence remains extremely vivid and even supportive. Jean Dominique, Céline, Kot,* and of course my mother and my father constantly remind me of how I should behave, of what my own values are. They give me courage.

Judy's senility throws me. There is no way to transcend it except through the memory of what she was. I suppose I have been honest about all the horror of senility because there are many people who have to face it alone. I have wished *to be present* to their pain. To be honest. Not to deny the physical facts which make transcendence difficult if not impossible. I have thought of those who share my pain, rather than of Judy who does not care, does not know, and is not in pain.

What of the nurses who deal with all this every day? How do they keep on being loving and care-full of a stranger who cannot respond? It takes superior love and superior detachment and I honor them for both, more than I can say. But for them there is the consolation of doing what has to be done, and they are not betrayed in their inmost hearts by what cannot be changed and can only get worse, as the families of loved ones are.

---

*S. S. Koteliansky

Monday, September 17th

THE REASON SENILITY is so frightening is, of course, that it shakes the foundations of our belief in what life is all about, a long process of growth, a ripening that we hope may be only one step in a long evolution of each soul towards more light. Senility destroys this illusion or appears to. When the self who makes connections goes, when there are no connections any more, how can one believe in a self that might go on somewhere else? But as I was considering this and sitting here, it occurred to me, and it was of comfort that atrophy, progressive arteriosclerosis of the brain, may not destroy what is stored there, but simply have frozen or stiffened it to where it is not *now* available. With the death of the body might it become available again? Who knows?

I have always believed that it is quite useless and in a way unsanctified to wish to probe the final mystery until we arrive there. I am disturbed and do not really like the idea of the psychic who believes he or she can reach the dead and communicate with them. I feel we have to live every moment, here and now, to the full and leave it to God as to where we are bound at the very end. If there is nothing, then all the more reason to make something as beautiful as possible out of each moment, to live it to the full.

The incredibly radiant days go on. Last evening the ocean was pure pale satin blue, perfectly quiet, and inside

the house the light at sunset was so rich and gold, I
thought when I went downstairs that I must have left
electric light burning!

But it was not a good or fulfilled day for the simple
reason that I got up an hour later than usual, at seven
instead of six, and so felt frantic trying to catch up on
letters the whole morning. It is worth everything to me
to feel the morning opening gently, not to be hurried, not
to push myself from one kind of response to another at top
speed.

Even Chausson, the tender melancholy of his music,
did not get me into a fruitful mood. And I did not find it
again until I went to bed and went on reading Mrs. Pandit's autobiography. Her description of the changes in life
style that rich cultivated Brahmins willingly made for the
sake of Gandhi's principles and in the struggle for Indian
independence is striking. Overnight decisions had to be
made to take all the beautiful saris out and burn them, to
wear only homespun, and to spend hours every day spin-
ning and weaving oneself, to give up the food one had
been accustomed to eating since childhood, and in Mrs.
Pandit's case to go out into the villages with her husband
and teach, and to face the possibility and then the reality
of imprisonment for months and years at a time. That is
a little of what independence cost and that millions of
people paid it willingly is cause for astonishment and
should make us here in the United States humble and
ashamed. Sometimes I think we are so silted up by material needs—or what we imagine to be needs—that we can
scarcely breathe. What a tremendous price we pay in true
freedom for every single thing we possess, or are pos-
sessed by! We are going to be buried alive one day in our
own waste—the endless catalogues that pour in, the horrendous amounts of food we throw away, the insane num-

bers of clothes we think we have to have. I feel especially guilty myself about the latter, as one result of the mastectomy was that I suddenly wanted new clothes, feminine clothes, as though they could make up for a lost breast! I am ashamed. But I can't help loving, nonetheless, a beautiful green velvet dress I ordered when in that mood.

Occasionally machines, those creations that I find most maddening, which I feel are my natural-born enemies, can perform a small miracle. This happened the other day when I unwrapped a large package from Dorothy Koeberlin in Washington. We have never met but we have corresponded for years, so it was an extraordinary moment when I found in that package a tape recorder and a cassette bringing me her deep true voice, and especially her wonderful laughter as, now she is recovering from an operation on her eyes, she "spoke" me a letter. And yesterday I put in a blank cassette and answered her. I read some of the new poems so she would know about the new book and could hear the music of these poems. This morning it will go off all the way to Washington answering her voice with mine.

It is the first time I have been glad of a cassette. Usually I am dismayed when one arrives from a stranger in lieu of a letter, for the simple reason that I can read a letter in a few moments but the cassette demands at least a half hour of time and becomes a real intrusion into the web of whatever I am doing and trying to create on a given day.

Tuesday, September 18th

I HAVE THE FEELING these days of returning from a long
journey back to myself and my life here as it was two or
three years ago, of coming *home* into my own ethos at last
after a long interruption. So I wake full of excitement at
the morning before me and all I hope to do within its brief
hours. The golden autumnal days continue like a blessing,
although it is now very dry and I see leaves wilting even
on perennials. Yesterday afternoon I threw duties to the
winds and went out to water the clematis along the fence,
one of the glories of this place.

It took me several minutes to remember the name
"clematis" and this happens a lot these days. I had "cyclamen" on my lips, as though memory had punched the
wrong button and couldn't find the right one. It is maddening, and strangely enough, happens quite often when
it comes to naming a flower. Of course it is much worse
when I forget the name of a human being whom I know
well. People my age tell me they have the same problem,
which is comforting. By the time one is sixty-seven the
number of names of people, flowers, places, birds, stored
in the bank is immense, and that may be partly why. A
false start, as happened just now, is fatal. Like a long
stammer.

Raymond came while I was outdoors and cut the grass
on the terrace and around the big maple where it grows
lush and fast, quite a job when it is long and wet as it was

yesterday, but what a pleasure to see order come back. This is a formal garden and a formal garden has to be kept neat or it makes for a disturbance in the mind. I fed and watered the iris bed I weeded the other day and put a sack of sunflower seed shells on it as a mulch. Then I went in and cooked, first brownies for Eleanor Blair whom I go down to see tomorrow, then a casserole to use a small eggplant Heidi had brought me with the recipe, and finally I prepared baked apples to put in the oven for my supper. It was a happy afternoon of life-giving chores and finally I went out with the bowl where I had stirred the brownies and asked Raymond whether he was enough of a boy to want to lick it with a spoon. He was.

All afternoon in the back of my mind I was cogitating about a small disturbance that has raised questions, a phrase in a letter from an old friend of mine and former student about "your ambivalent generosities." It is true that I am ambivalent about what it takes to answer letters and also to see people and cook for them when I am struggling with a piece of work, as, I fear, I always am. Sometimes I even utter this conflict and of course that is not quite gentlemanly, but maybe we have to take on faith that in the end people do what they want to do, even when complaining that it is too much! Once more dear George Herbert comes to my rescue:

> I will complain, yet praise;
> I will bewail, approve:
> And all my sour-sweet days
> I will lament, and love.

As far as I can see from here almost everyone I know is trying to do the impossible every day. All mothers, all writers, all artists of every kind, every human being who has work to do and still wants to stay human and to be responsive to other human beings' needs, joys, and sorrows. There is never enough time and that's the rub. In my case every choice I make means depriving someone. I write one letter and have to push another aside. I go away for a few days to see a friend, and lose the thread of the journal.

What I came to see yesterday afternoon is how much imagination is needed to "take in" another's life and what it costs. We are very much aware of our own conflicts and often fail to understand those of someone else. No day passes now without some request for an opinion, for help in getting published (Oh, how I sympathize and long to help!). It's the old story. One thing one can do but when that thing is multiplied to an X number, it is a continuous drain on energy. I live in a perpetual state of guilt about the "undone." Probably everyone does?

But it may be easier, for instance, for a woman with a family to push guilt aside because she is doing the essential thing. The immediate need is her family. For me it is not as clear. How can I say my work is more important than the need for response of a perfect stranger who is dying of cancer, or terrified because she has fallen in love with a woman at fifty, though she is happily married, or in despair because his or her poems are turned down and where to turn? Everyone of these trusting and hopeful strangers needs and should get an immediate response. More often than not, they do.

But frustration piles up, too, and finally there is an outburst or a complaint which is thrown back at me as your "ambivalent generosities."

Wednesday, September 19th

I HAVE BEEN THINKING about the image of a journey as
the image for a love affair and its ending as the coming
home to one's self again. The value of loving someone
passionately, often a person very unlike oneself, is that
one is taken literally out of one's self on a journey into
unknown territory. As in a journey to a foreign country
there is culture shock; one often feels lonely, even attacked by the differences. One is also all the time in a state
of strange excitement, there are glorious moments, unfor-
gettable scenes that make one tremble with joy and surprise, and there are days of great fatigue when all one
longs for is home, to be with the familiar that does not ask
for stretching to understand it, which can be taken for
granted. Where one can rest. And above all where one is
accepted as one is, not stammering in an unfamiliar language, not trying desperately to communicate from one
ethos to another.

For a week or more I have been in a state of extreme
excitement, as though on the brink of revelation. It began
at once as soon as I had decided to bring myself to the
point of decision and to break off, not to cling out of need
and desperation to something that perhaps was never
there. The central person focuses the world and when
there is no one to be that, one is at first terrified. But once
the decision is made that had to be made, one is free at
last to go home to the self, that self which has been cen-

sored, without even being aware of it, by the effort to please and to become acceptable to the one one loves. Now I believe we can be friends in a clearer air, she and I.

One of the censors that has been at work has been the notion that to be in love at our age is ludicrous and somehow not proper, that passionate love can be banished after sixty shall we say? That is one of the myths that has been around a long time, but it was never true. Love at any age has its preposterous side—that is why it comes as a kind of miracle at any age. It is never commonplace, never to be experienced without a tremor. But to stop arbitrarily the flow of life because of a preconceived idea, any preconceived idea, is to damage the truth of the inner person . . . that is dangerous. Are we not on earth to love each other? And to grow? And how does one grow except through love, except through opening ourselves to other human beings to be fertilized and made new?

Wednesday, September 26th

I HAVE BEEN AWAY for a few days in Center Sandwich, New Hampshire, at Huldah's, an uplifting taste of mountains and lakes, and those charming woodsy roads, still unpaved, that remind me of Nelson. Huldah invited Tamas, so he had a fine holiday with us and her two big collies. All my feeling for New England returned as I drove along on my way there, though the season is not advanced and only a few swamp maples were scarlet.

What I thought, not for the first time, was that there is nowhere, perhaps, in the world where one sees so many distinguished small houses, and this surely has something to do with the character of the people who built them. In the South there are magnificent "great houses," but small houses are apt to be shabby and architecturally nondescript. All along the road by Lake Winnipesaukee I passed small white houses with sparkling many-paned windows and beautifully designed doorways often with a huge barn attached or beside them, the shingles weathered dove gray—what dreams they evoke of another life, though it is a life I lived once for fifteen years in Nelson. However, the country around Center Sandwich is more beautiful, on a grander scale, than that in the Monadnock region. There are many ranges making a strong elegant profile against the sky wherever one turns, and many rich brooks tumbling over smooth granite stones, so the sound of water is never far away, an intimate sound, very different from that of the ocean.

When I reached Huldah's house I kept listening and was startled by the total silence, not a bird singing or a cricket chirping for the first hours I was there. And I realized finally that what made the silence so immense was the absence of the ocean, and how much I missed it, and also the constant cries of gulls and the wood pigeons cooing and the goldfinches' delightful running cheeps in flight.

How marvelous to live in a world where all this is within reach, gentle mountains, clear lakes, and the ocean! New England. Its essence is a fine mixture of grandeur—the natural scene—and intimacy, the small much lived-in house where one sits by the fire in a room lined with books.

In the four days there were two peak experiences as Maslow would name them. One was late in the afternoon when the sun suddenly touched a bowl of lavender colchicum (they appear to be huge crocuses and bloom in the autumn) on the sill in Huldah's big room. In the slanting light they became transparent, lavender flames. They seemed to gather all the light into themselves, centering for a few moments the whole world so nothing else existed. A moment of ecstasy.

The other peak experience came after a splendid walk to Dog Cove—a walk through great trees, moss underfoot and the leaves of many wildflowers to note, mushrooms, great lichen-covered rocks looming up, and the broken light through birch and ash leaves, and through white pine. Huldah's collies move about all this with great elegance in their white ruffs on their long legs. Tamas, more sedate, trundles ahead, like a small animated barrel of fur. The path leads finally to Squam Lake and a series of small white birches . . . lovely when one glimpses the shining blue through the trees. There we spread a blanket and had our picnic, fish chowder and a great salad of hard-boiled eggs, lettuce and blue cheese with French dressing, and a Bartlett pear.

And then the silence fell.

We simply sat there and drank in the dappled water, a couple of gulls swimming around a big rock, and far away a pine-covered island and beyond that rising up in the distance the deep blue rounded peaks of the Sandwich range. How rare in our world to sit absolutely still for an hour, not thinking, not even feeling, simply being in the presence of great beauty! At first one notices the small things, the subtle changes as wind suddenly ruffles a small space in the water, the amber color of still water over sand, or the reflection of a single tree, but little by little, it is the whole unified scene that takes over. And it is the silence itself that unifies it. One slides down deep deep into contemplation. This is not ecstasy like the light on lavender petals. It is more like prayer. Beauty beyond our understanding and beyond our uniqueness as individuals. Presence that asks nothing of us except to be in its presence. And filled with that presence we walked back into our separate lives.

Thursday, September 27th

PAIN IS THE GREAT TEACHER. I woke before dawn with this thought. Joy, happiness, are what we take and do not question. They are beyond question, maybe. A matter of being. But pain forces us to think, and to make connections, to sort out what is what, to discover what has been happening to cause it. And, curiously enough, pain draws us to other human beings in a significant way, whereas joy or happiness to some extent, isolates.

I was accused the other day by a good friend of mine of loving to suffer, of enjoying pain, as though it were really my climate. I don't believe this for a minute because in every single day of my life I experience so many joys, such as yesterday planting twenty-four daffodils here and there, while Raymond was clearing out the border below the terrace. Every now and then I raised my head and met the incredible soft blue ocean, each time startled into consciousness that it is an extraordinary blessing to live within its presence.

It is not that I choose pain or wish it . . . I am not crazy, after all! But I do know that pain, which is usually caused by our relations with each other, has always been a means toward growth. When we speak of being vulnerable, it suggests being especially vulnerable to pain. People for whom personal dignity and self-sufficiency are everything do all they can to shut it out. *Noli me tangere.* They are well aware that any intimate relationship has pain in it, forces a special kind of awareness, is costly, and so they try to keep themselves unencumbered by shutting pain out as far as it is possible to do so.

The examination of pain does not come from self-pity, nor does being willing to experience it for the sake of personal truth mean one is masochistic. For one cannot probe pain or come to terms with what it has to teach without detachment. It is the sentimentalists who cannot bear to look at their pain, who wallow in it, and it is the cowards who simply shut it out by refusing to experience it.

Pain is the great teacher if we can look at it coldly, examine it as a doctor examines a broken arm. It comes almost always I think from a dysjunction, or a non-meeting of some sort. We feel misunderstood and react accordingly by an attack on the one who has misunderstood. Anger is nearly always a reaction to hurt. After the episode, two people have been wounded, and there is dysjunction.

What has happened?

Friday, September 28th

I WAS INTERRUPTED YESTERDAY just as I had asked that question, "what has happened?" and never got back to it. Things have piled up here, but I long to get back to some quiet thinking.

When we delve down and discover what has happened, the source of the pain, it almost always requires facing two things, one the part one's own faults have played in the dilemma, the dysjunction, and the other the necessity to enlarge one's understanding and compassion by once more "taking in the stranger." These are acts of the spirit and they are never easy to make. Pride has to go first, self-righteousness has to go, the need to be "right" has to go.

We are all stubborn creatures at heart and very little radical change can be expected of us, at least after sixty. But what can change is *understanding*. The dark side of a temperament or of a nature will always be there, but what one hopes is to understand it better, and to make allowances, but we have to forgive ourselves before we can forgive others. The light shed can be dazzling after a tussle with oneself, if one can come out forgiving. And that light heals.

For some reason I am reminded by all this of a letter Margaret Clapp wrote me in 1961 when I was teaching at Wellesley and that I came upon by chance the other day. She wrote, "I am delighted to have your poems, some of them old friends, some new to me . . . and to have them from you. But 'not to rebel against what pulls us down'* —this is not in this world. Maybe in another era we can argue it out, for now, I have time, alas, not even to rebel. I am convinced that discipline helps, but grace is what matters. And contrary to the fathers, I suspect grace, though it cannot be earned, must be earned to be conferred."

When grace is given it comes to us as joy, maybe, but it can also be earned, I am convinced, through the rigorous examination of the sources of pain.

Monday, October 1st

MY DEAR OLD FRIENDS, Christiane and Vincent Hepp, whom I haven't seen for two years, not since their oldest son, Olivier, died suddenly at twenty-one of an aneurism, have been here for twenty-four rich hours. They were due to arrive around three but got lost and finally drove up in the gentle gray mist at around five. Because my study here is on the third floor where I cannot see the driveway I hesitated to come up and write letters as I would have done in Nelson while waiting for guests. But in a way those two hours gave me the rare pleasure of loafing, and of looking around my house and enjoying it all by myself.

Meanwhile I did some small chores like polishing the tarnished teapot, bringing up wood. Mostly I lay on the

*"Somersault," Sarton. *Collected Poems*

chaise longue on the porch and watched the chickadees, back again after the summer, and the purple finches and nuthatches making their spiralling flights in and out of the feeders in the cherry tree at the window. Suspense, waiting, tenses one up. Certain perceptions are intensified— it is beautiful to look through from the porch to the cosy room where my eyes rest on mother's big desk, and then across the hall and into the library to be fortified by the Bahut with its strength and beauty glowing in the distance. I love the spaces in this house, its amplitude.

These are melancholy days because the weather has changed. The sea is gray, the colors just coming into their peak are subdued, "season of mists and mellow fruitfulness." But perhaps it was right and matched our mood, the Hepps and I.

What a joy to be with people who can express (in their beautiful French) so many shades and depths of experience! We drank champagne by the fire in the library, as we always do. At one point Vincent spoke of how rarely in the United States are people able to ask the right questions, to draw a guest out, that they often felt among their Connecticut neighbors unable to feel themselves as *existing,* because on social occasions so little of value is called out. Is it shyness, I wonder? In France "la politesse" is taught, or used to be, and the art of conversation is part of it. Here in America it is sometimes possible to talk "shop" (but rarely if the "shop" is as intangible as writing as a profession) but I have been dismayed lately to realize how often "conversation" becomes simply discussing the cost of living, the weather, or food. I have wondered whether I was insensitive to mind, or arrogant to believe that I have thoughts worth drawing out and am eager to listen to some talk about real things. It was consoling to hear that the Hepps have had the same impression.

I watched Vincent's lean distinguished face, the quiet intensity of his being, and listened to his always gentle voice as he turns over in his mind and accompanies one on a journey of discovery on some point of interest such as this one about conversation. He has such a distinguished mind, and (far rarer) such a finely tuned sensibility. And I looked across at Christiane, at her warm beauty, those brilliant blue eyes, where tears sometimes stand, her natural outspoken character, her style . . . what a waste that such gifts have gone unused, at least on the social plane!

It occurred to me as we talked that not only are American young people never taught how to make conversation, but also never taught how to write letters, how one must try to encompass the other person and his or her life, while at the same time offering one's own, and that all adds up to bridging a distance, to making a superior kind of contact that nourishes. All this has nothing to do with intellect or education, really. Some of the best letters I ever get are from Gracie Warner in Nelson, telling me of the goings-on at the farm, speaking of her most intimate friends, the ponies, the single old sheep, the goats, the pheasants, the Muscovy ducks. A whole world comes to life between the lines, as does her concern that I am well, far away over the hills by the sea.

Of course when I see Vincent we always speak of his remarkable mother, Marianne Hepp, known as a writer by her pen name Camille Mayran, a writer who won the Femina Vie Heureuse prize years ago for her novel, *Dame en Noir.* I met her at the Huxleys' in 1936 and we have corresponded ever since. I don't believe anyone has ever read my poems with more understanding or appreciated them more. Vincent told me about the celebration last January of her ninetieth birthday, how perfectly herself she is at that great age, and I thought that this is the only instance in my life where I have been as intimate with a mother and a son, and how precious an interweaving that can be. And we talked of their two remaining children, Guillaume, at nineteen taking a year off before college, and at the moment working as dishwasher on a huge oil rig in New Jersey to earn enough to go to Peru and Brazil, his dream. And of Florence who has gone to Japan as a visitor, hoping to find a job and be able to stay there for a year.

But it was not until after breakfast the next morning that we were able to touch the wound, the loss of Olivier. We had come back from a walk through the sodden woods and down to the sea where we stood watching the surf lace itself about the rocks, we had come back to the cold hearth in the library for an hour's talk before they had to leave. It seemed natural then to ask the questions I had held back. One of the hardest things, Christiane said, was that for the first three weeks they were never alone. Kind neighbors constantly came and went, bringing food, being supportive in the usual ways, but I could sense that under all that was a desperate need for simple grief, and to be alone to experience it, to weep those tears of despair alone. One of the people who helped most was a woman doctor who felt such outrage at this senseless death of a glowingly alive young man that she could not come and see them for three weeks, she herself was in such shock.

There are some griefs that will never heal and in the presence of them the only comfort perhaps is to recognize that fact. As tears poured down Christiane's cheeks, I remembered the wisdom of the Pueblo Indians who allow six months of mourning and then free the spirits of the dead and themselves with a dance. This led us into talking about the absence of rites in our civilization and that we

need them badly. The Pope's visit has brought this home, for surely it was the combination of a rite that has continued to be performed for two thousand years, suddenly made fresh and given to us as a new communion because of this man's character and charisma, that has created such enthusiasm and lifted so many people into recognizing a spiritual universe.

Saturday, October 6th

OH LIFE! Too much is happening all at once and I have no time to sort it all out. Today the children from Acton who have been coming, for a picnic for the past four years and are now in Junior High (I can't believe it!) are coming, and thank goodness we have a dark blue sea and a shining day after a deluge last night.

Since my last entry Huldah has been here for two splendid days which included a morning of planting bulbs and a glorious walk down the empty Ogunquit Beach with her two collies and Tamas. It was a muted day, warm, the ocean, slate gray that turned blue as we walked back, the dogs in an ecstasy at this huge empty space in which to run, and I in an ecstasy at the immemorial beauty of this immense beach . . . it was all luminous so even the ugly row of houses in the distance were lit up as in an impressionist painting. A very few people walking and a few sedate gulls standing about punctuated the scene, so timeless it might have been sixty years ago when I spent summers here as a child with my parents.

On Wednesday Huldah and I and the three dogs set out for Patsy Carlson's house on an island near Damariscotta for two days of island living and its special pleasures. I have missed Greenings Island since Anne Thorp's death so I savored every moment. It is the classic Maine scene of fir-covered rocky islands strewn about a bay, each mysterious and unique as an individual human being, each with one or two houses one glimpses through the trees, and the great rocks worn smooth by wave and tide along the edges, lobster pots bobbing about everywhere, of course. On the first day we walked for an hour through the mossy, mushroom-dotted woods along the town road, which is really a wide grassy path. There are no cars on the island, only a few tractors for hauling, so it is very silent and wild feeling. Only an occasional rush of dogs broke the stillness as Patsy's went flying past and Tamas on his short legs tried to catch her, and as Huldah's big collies, waving their plumed tails appeared and disappeared in and out of the wood—benign presences.

Sunday, October 7th

TIME HAS COLLAPSED like one of those collapsing drinking cups that fold away in a picnic basket because of all the events of these past days and I must try to catch the essence of our island trip.

The single image that will stay with me is our crossing the bay to a cove on Cranberry Island. From a distance we could see three elegant pines standing on a jetty of

smoothed amber rocks—all through this landscape there
are visual incidents that resemble Japanese prints and this
was one. Patsy slowed the motor, and we glided into a
perfect semi-circle, a cove between two embracing rocky
points. Before us, a small sandy beach, edged with pines
and a few deciduous trees showing yellow and orange
through the dark greens. It was like a dream, so perfectly
"arranged," so perfectly quiet. Once seen, it will always
be there in the mind, a Maine lyric.

Harder to encompass but no less beautiful was a long
walk we took through the woodsy road and across the
island, Patsy noting mushrooms of every color and kind,
picking a wintergreen berry for us to taste, or a ground
blackberry, or pointing out the dark leaves and red berries of the holly just fruiting. The floor of these woods is
a tapestry of color and form, the lichened rocks standing
out among flat spaces covered with the silvery gray of the
deer moss, and the round emerald humps of that other
moss I used to capture for Japanese gardens in a bowl,
fallen leaves in their browns and golds, sheets of deep
brown bracken, and once a tree covered with a wild
grapevine heavy with grapes. Small asters everywhere.
After the big rain of the night before, the road became a
pool to be waded now and then. The dogs drank their way
through happily, while we tried for a foothold on the
mossy edge.

Every now and then the landscape changed to a place
of small silver birches, elegant and airy, or a dense pine
wood, big trees and no underbrush, or a cleared field with
ancient apple trees standing about the ruins of a house.
The mushroomy, piney, rotting-leaf smell was always
there. At last we came out to blue water and a grand
empty hunting lodge where I was glad to sit down for a
half hour, and very relieved when the young caretaker, a

friend of Patsy's, offered to take us home by water, all seven of us, four dogs and three people, in a whaler.

"Messing about in boats" is of course one of the chief activities of island life. It was grand that evening to embark again for a drink at the Flints down the island, and to come back as the full moon was rising over a calm sea.

In two days we had a sampler of Maine weather. The night before there had been a wild storm of rain, thunder, and lightning, that day clear skies, and on the day we left a magic but dangerous blanket of fog through which pine trees suddenly appeared and then disappeared as we were ferried back to the continent, dogs, luggage and all by Patsy's jack-of-all-trades who knows every rock and reef by heart. Still, it was rather a relief when the float on the mainland loomed up and we knew we were safe.

Monday, October 7th

LONGING FOR A SPELL of bright blue days, we are being teased by alternate days of rain . . . today, a blue sky and high wind, to be followed we are told by rain again tomorrow. I had hoped to plant bulbs yesterday afternoon, but it began to rain at three and that was that. In a housekeeping fit, inspired no doubt by Patsy's shining house, I cleaned the two copper jugs in the library, and the brass Cape Cod lighter. Guests are a stimulus in such matters and tomorrow Huldah brings her niece, Ann Street, to lunch from Center Sandwich. I am cross about the expected rain, but happy to welcome Ann here at last. She is a portrait painter and has the painter's eye so I trust the shining copper will be noted.

I am enjoying a day of solitude after all the comings and goings lately.

I have to write a five-minute speech I must give at a dinner honoring Muriel Rukeyser next week in New York. A short speech is the hardest kind, and it is better on such occasions not to be too serious, so I may praise Muriel for an odd reason. Years ago during World War II we lived across the street from each other on West 10th Street in New York; we were each working at OWI, she as head of the poster division and I as a writer of documentary films for propaganda. Among many other things, I learned from her that loafing is not a crime, that to lie around reading magazines and appearing to do nothing can be a very good idea. I had been brought up in a household where work was the redeemer, brought up to forgive my father for his faults as a human being because of his great work. Work, I discovered early on, excuses one from some sins. Muriel has produced a large opus of poems and prose works but as her work time is late at night, she often loafs in the daytime. This trait amazed, amused, and finally convinced me. Being "active," "doing something" may be an escape from loafing for when one loafs the imagination springs into being and all kinds of unexpected things may happen in the psyche. Compulsive "doers" are at least sometimes deliberately escaping themselves, or their *selves*.

But before I find a humorous way to praise Muriel, I think about how great she has become since suffering two strokes. There is now a refinement, a subtleizing of her Buddha-like face, a gentleness, an acceptance that reminded me, when I saw her in a documentary film last year, of the portrait of Isak Dinesen by Cecil Beaton that sits on my mother's desk in the cosy room. She is sitting with a small formal bunch of flowers in her hands and she is smiling, "My life, I will not let you go except thou bless me, but then I will let you go." In the portrait she has let go with an air of bliss, of angelic acceptance—and three days later she was dead.

But before I come to Muriel this morning I must add a word about Patsy's house. It has the feel of a promise kept or a long dream that has come true, and here Patsy's gift for organizing—she was a career woman in New York, then rather late in life married a diplomat and found herself entertaining on a large scale as wife of our ambassador to Colombia—achieves a kind of perfection. It is as though here she had been able to express her inner life, her childlike love of flowers for instance, as a poet might have done by writing poems. Maybe one has to be a child in some way to live happily on an island where a great deal of time is spent hauling things in and out in a boat, concocting picnics, bringing in wood for the big open fireplace, and cooking for innumerable guests. Patsy is happy and that in itself shows a kind of genius, and is reflected in her house, so full of light and space, airy and immaculate.

Wednesday, October 10th

AFTER SO MANY DOINGS it takes a while to resume myself
alone. When Huldah and Ann had gone yesterday afternoon—they had left Center Sandwich in a small blizzard!
—the house felt huge and empty, and I lay around for an
hour reading magazines in that limbo between lives. I had
hoped to be able to plant bulbs, impossible in driving rain,
but the other day in a high wind I did manage to get about
a hundred in, tulips, narcissi and grape hyacinths. So that
is something.

It was lovely to see Ann's enthusiasm yesterday—it
gave me back my first excitement about the place when
I moved in six years ago. For her, with a family of her own
and parents still alive, with her career as portrait painter,
and a busy social life, I could feel that the beauty and
spaciousness of the house, the great presence of the
ocean, and solitude above all, were enviable. It *is* a kind
of heaven-haven and I glowed in the reflection of her
delight.

Friday, October 12th

I BEGAN THIS JOURNAL ten months ago as a way of getting
back to my self, of pulling out of last year's depression, and
now I am truly on a rising curve. What has changed in a
miraculous way is the landscape of the heart, so somber
and tormented for over a year that I was not myself. Did
letting go last month do it? What has happened, that quite
suddenly some weeks ago the landscape became luminous and peaceful, no anger, no irritation, as though the
screen that had separated us for so long had simply lifted
away as fog sometimes does in these parts? Whatever the
cause it feels like a miracle. Perhaps Agape has entered
the scene and driven manic-depressive, neurotically de-
pendent Eros away. I feel blest in my love, and able to
give blessing as a result.

So it is time for a pause in these reflections and to
welcome joy and praise back, so long absent.

Thursday, October 18th

I FEEL LIKE A PACK RAT, I have come home with such a various complex bundle of experience to recount and to sort out after two days in New York. How beautiful to be able to do it on such a still, radiant autumnal day, only a faint murmur of ocean and a diffused light, a few birds shrieking at the feeder—jays, I expect—and then the silence. I have to listen hard to detect the faint susurration of the sea against the rocks.

I had gone down for two reasons. The first was the dinner in honor of Muriel Rukeyser at the Pierre on the fifteenth. I felt extremely nervous, an old raccoon wandering into such a grand hotel (I have never been there before) dazzled by the lights. I am so rarely dressed up that that too made me nervous, a new, green crushed-velvet dress, and the little fur coat I bought in Dallas years ago and almost never wear, seemed a disguise. By that I mean I did manage to look like everyone else in the lobby as I walked in, not conspicuously out of place as I felt. I had to go through the bar to reach the dining room, and there I found Erica Jong having a drink alone. We were each nervous about the speeches we had to make at the dinner, so it was good to have a little talk together before we went in. She had that very day handed in the seven hundred and fifty pages of her new novel, and for a good half hour we exchanged lives and anxieties. How young she looks, a delightful being. But at last we had to go and meet the other circus animals gathered around the bar in the dinner room. There was Eberhart, rosy and ebullient as ever, and tall Ned O'Gorman whom I have long regarded as a saint because of his work in Harlem. For fourteen years, he told me, he has gone there every day to the storefront where he shelters and nourishes preschool blacks who would otherwise be playing in the gutters. In honor of Muriel he was in black tie, and I expect he, like me, felt in disguise. I am so rarely among fellow poets that it was a great treat to talk with old friends, as we waited for Muriel to arrive. And finally there she was, erect and smiling in a long dress, so much herself—that wonderful Buddha smile—that it was hard to believe that it is a real effort for her now to take a single step. She moved on two canes very slowly toward her table, her son, and Bill Meredith, at her side. Of course I went right over once she was seated and for five minutes we were back at West 10th Street, laughing as we remembered that other life, thirty-four years ago.

What a pleasure it was to find myself seated beside Jane Cooper whom I had never met, but whose work has always spoken to me as few of her contemporaries do, and beside her, Helen Adams, the writer of extraordinary ballads, whom I also had never laid eyes on before. M. L. Rosenthal sat at my left and we had a cosy happy time.

Clearly we were having such a good time because this has always been the atmosphere Muriel creates. Gathered to celebrate her, we were encircled by it, an atmosphere of a special kind of joy, which is exemplified by the way Muriel says "hello" in her soft voice, as though whomever she addresses were being welcomed to a feast, as though something wonderful were about to happen, as though the air was full of miracles.

And the speeches, made from a small stage right in front of Muriel's table, were brief and deeply felt, not at all the boring longueurs such occasions usually bring about. But, then, poets are used to economy in words. I liked best Bill Meredith's because he had the wit to make four or five quotations from Muriel herself, and I was happy that my guess that a little humor would not be out of place proved right.

I got back to the Cosmopolitan Club before ten and lay in my bed with the French doors open onto the lighted towers of New York, awake for a long time. It was beautiful but also a little frightening when I thought how much energy it cost, must cost, to keep this magical city lit and warm. It boggles the imagination to conceive of all that energy.

Next morning Bill Packard came at ten to interview me for the *New York Quarterly* (the sponsors of Muriel's dinner) about lyric poetry. I enjoyed talking about it, and am grateful for his questions, and for his having taken the trouble to read the *Collected Poems,* bringing with him a heavily marked-up copy. What is more flattering than a marked-up copy of a book?

After that I had lunch at the Algonquin with Eric Swenson, my editor at Norton, and Tim Seldes, my agent. We had to talk a little about the great race in England earlier this summer when some boats capsized and Eric's made it to the end—what an adventure! Tim has a fine hard edge. It's refreshing, and reminded me of Diarmuid Russell, whose agency he has taken over. Eric is the only person I have ever known who appears to have no *angst.* He is always merry, confident that all will be well, and a great support. The contract on the poems has gone through, and I gather that Norton will gladly advance me something on this journal in early January so I can pay my taxes and not starve. It is a close thing this year, because I have had no book out.

But the day was rising on a long curve toward the first showing of the film interview, "World of Light, a Portrait of May Sarton," the second reason why I had come to New York. I just had time to go to the club for a short rest before finding my way back again to the dear old Algonquin for a drink with Doris Grumbach, and then to walk to 1600 Broadway for the showing. Doris came up from Washington to see it and hold my hand. I must say, I was rather nervous at the idea that so much of the inner person was about to be made visible before an audience of whom I was one, not only the person inside but also the bulky person outside!

This showing was for friends of Martha Wheelock and Marita Simpson who made the film; Eric and Tim Seldes were there as well as Doris, and Jean Burden, briefly in New York, was able to come too. As soon as the room was dark and all the dear faces blotted out we were transported to York, watching the sunrise from my bedroom. From then on, I knew all would be well. Martha and Marita have done a superb job and because it is a work of art I could look at myself rather objectively, and be delightfully surprised by what they managed to draw out of me, how close to the marrow much of it is, and, from a visual point of view, how well they have evoked the beauty of this place. Near the end I read "Gestalt at Sixty" and while I read, magnificent images of Nelson and the hills and lakes are shown, then the tide rising here on the rocks in lacy foam. There is a walk with Tamas and Bramble and there are beautiful evocations, like Dutch paintings, of various rooms in this house. All Martha's and Marita's hard work, and long hours in the editing room have borne a beautiful fruit.

Last night, thinking it all over, too tired and excited to sleep, I did have a moment of quiet panic at how much of me has been given away in this film, and understood the fear primitive people have of the camera. But I decided that one does not lose one's soul for giving it away.

Tuesday, October 23rd

WE ARE HAVING A HEAT WAVE. I set out for Center Sandwich on Sunday in summer clothes, with Tamas panting beside me. I had expected all the leaves to be gone so far West and North, but at Wolfeboro I found myself in a golden world . . . the red maples have no leaves but the yellow ones were in full glory and the beeches at peak took my breath away, all this gold against hazy blue sky, and the lake almost lost in the mist. In York we have missed the autumn glory, but there it was in full spate, the mountains a sumptuous tapestry of purple and crimson in the distance. What luck to have such a twenty-four hours before Huldah goes back to Tennessee!

I was home again yesterday around noon, the temperature 80°, and some last roses in bloom to welcome me back. I picked a small bowl of raspberries, and freshened up the flowers in the house. It is always the "rite" of coming home to water the plants in the plant window and rearrange the flowers in jars and vases, a way of landing and rooting myself again.

I lay on the *chaise longue* watching the birds at the feeder and reading the mail, among it one of those re-

markable letters from Vincent Hepp which are always for
me "occasions" to be reread and meditated upon, rare
occasions, occasions for rejoicing. In this one he speaks of
the visit of John Paul.

How magnificent! How truly a visitor! . . . Paul came to see us,
to touch us, each one of us, with no other purpose. A visit is to
meditate on our great joy of being alive, of standing, walking,
running on the face of this planet, of seeping in the soft miracle
of light, amid the trees and the birds and the goats and all our
brothers and sisters in creation. Yes, he was strong and virile in
proclaiming those simple truths, while the wise and worldly of
the political scene appear so unsure, so irresolute, and so cow-
ardly!

I came back to that and also to the newspapers and the
horrendous sights of Cambodian starvation on television
last night. If only the Pope's message on that score could
penetrate, the necessity for the sharing by all of us in the
rich countries with those in the poor ones, to take up that
burden as the most essential, for in the long run we *are*
all one family on the earth, and when some members
starve we shall, in the end, pay a high price for their
neglect. I feel the Pope did make clear and in a wonderful
way this human unity . . . it is too bad that he failed to
include women in the church as part of it. For there he
was of no comfort, and indeed created dismay.

Lying there for an hour on the *chaise longue* I found
Hans Kung's moving analysis "Pope John Paul II: His First
Year" in the *Times* of Friday, October 19th. I want to
think about this.

Wednesday, October 24th

HEIDI CAME AT NOON yesterday and, amazing grace, it was so warm we had our drinks outside on the terrace, looking out over the bronzes and golds of the bushes and vines on the terrace wall, down the field to a hazy gray-blue sea. A cardinal flew in to eat the berries of the andromeda, such an event! and Heidi was fascinated when we went indoors for oyster stew to see the birds so near the table, in the ornamental cherry just outside the window. It is decorative now, as the leaves are dark purplish bronze and the bunches of cherries, small chartreuse globes. At lunch time the air is full of wings, then an interval while the red squirrel comes flying in. Even jays are afraid of her and eventually I pound on the window to give the birds a chance.

The whole of Hans Kung's essay on the Pope's first year is remarkable. The gist of it as follows: (Op Ed Page, N.Y. Times, Oct. 19th)

And he especially sees the commitment of his person and office for the repressed and underprivileged people of the world as his special duty and responsibility.

Nevertheless, it must now be added that many people within and without the Catholic Church ask:

Does this commitment toward the outside, the world, also correspond to a commitment toward the inside, the church, the ecclesiastical institution itself?

Can a message to the world to change be credible

if the Pope and the church themselves are not the first to change in their own praxis, even, and especially where they themselves are most challenged?

Can the Pope and the church credibly speak to the conscience of today's people, if a self-critical examination of conscience on the part of the church and its leadership does not simultaneously occur, with the irksome consequences this might imply?

Is talk of a fundamental renewal of human society credible when the doctrinal and practical reform of the church with respect to the head and the members does not also decisively continue, and when irksome inquiries (as for example concerning the population explosion, birth control and ecclesiastical infallibility) are not finally taken seriously and honestly responded to?

Kung closes with this statement.

But after all, we should affirm in our Catholic Church the words of Gregory the Great (590–604), one of the luminous predecessors of Pope John Paul II:
'But if the truth causes scandal, then it is better a scandal rather than that the truth be abandoned.'

The Pope has experienced the fight for human rights in his own life under the communists in Poland, and has felt this on his pulse. It may be that his lack of interest and concern toward women as mothers, as potential priests, as sexually enslaved by men (where there is no sanction for birth control) is quite simply that these are things he cannot have experienced "on the pulse." He is human, after all.

Friday, October 26th

HOW ASTOUNDING to find a last cupful of raspberries yesterday afternoon, and to pick a few last asters and nasturtiums and two roses in bud! It is true October weather now and I had expected to find every sign of life frozen solid, so, instead of fertilizing the perennial border as I had planned to do, I arranged three tiny bunches of flowers, recovering slowly from a luncheon guest. There is someone coming for lunch every day this week, so it made me smile to read in the fifth volume of Virginia Woolf's letters, "I've seen too many humans, and would like a long dose of donkeys." I hate to finish that book, and have prolonged doing so by rationing it to a few pages at a time. In another passage, this time a letter to Ethel Smyth, the composer, V. W. speaks of writing letters,

> I'm sorry I've been so incommunicative, but I can only write letters when my mind is full of bubble and foam; when I'm not aware of the niceties of the English language. You don't know the bother it is, using for one purpose what I'm perpetually using for another. Could you sit down and improvise a dance at the piano after tea to please your friends? And now, home here, I shall drink no more wine—now we're landed and are strewn with bills, letters, manuscripts, dark men from the East who must see Leonard— etc. etc. I can't count the number of flies on this dead horse.

It's really always the same problem, too much of anything, even food, deadens and appalls. The quality of life depends on small amounts of fully experienced or "taken in" material for the senses and the mind. So answering one real letter is a pleasure, for someone living alone a good way of being in relation to another human being, but answering or knowing that one must eventually answer a hundred (my present state) becomes a nightmare. All through this year of reevaluating and coming to terms with my life, of building back a sense of identity and purpose after being badly thrown, I have known that before the end of this year and of this journal I would have to make it known to myself and my correspondents that I am making a radical decision not to answer letters from readers and/or strangers any longer. Such letters must be taken gratefully as answers to a piece of work, to a poem or a novel. They must be taken and enjoyed without guilt. Well, it is easy to say this, to say it at last after months of wondering how and when I could do so, but I know it is not going to be easy to do! However, when eighty percent of work time goes into responding to others, something "has to give."

Tuesday, October 30th

IN A WEEK OF SEEING PEOPLE I miss writing in the journal. I am now beginning to revise and get the manuscript ready for Nancy Hartley who is typing it, fifty pages at a time, so already it is leaving me and being read by some-

one else, a strange feeling always and this time stranger than ever before with a journal, for although the reasons for keeping it are somewhat the same as they were for *Journal of a Solitude* —recovery from depression, and the facing up to the end of a love affair—this time the long game of solitaire is "coming out" in several beautiful ways. This time I have recovered the sense of myself without losing love. That is the miracle, that my lover and I have come through together to a place of benign peace and light. Miracles cannot be explained, that is their miraculous nature. They are beyond ratiocination, so I cannot tell what has really happened. But I know we have reached haven and can see each other clearly in all our differences and enjoy each other for what each of us is at last.

At the same time seeing the documentary film in New York has restored me to a sense of what my life is all about, and that I do have value as a human being and as a writer. What a gift that has been from Martha and Marita and Ishtar (the name of their firm), Ishtar, the goddess who has surely helped this dream of theirs to come true.

When I was at the lowest ebb in April of this year, I asked Karen Saum whether she would like to consider coming to live with me here through the winter months. She agreed to do so as an experiment on both sides, and she comes day after tomorrow, November 1st, to begin the experiment. I have the warm excitement that mothers must feel when a daughter is coming home to stay for a time, the joy it is to think of making our supper, of going down as the light fades not to the solitude of magazines and TV as the end to the day, but to a dear smiling face, and someone with whom to exchange the day's inner adventures. That is what I have missed. The telephone is no substitute though I use it freely to call friends as far away as New Mexico and Tennessee. But there the danger is that the imperious ring startles the answerer out of a mood or a task, interrupts in a crude way whatever is going on at the other end. Woe and tears or anger may pour out and throw everything off kilter.

I decided to ask Karen to come when a dear friend told me "I can't take your moods on the telephone." The phone had been the lifeline, but I realized that it was not fair to use it as a lifeline, so the solution appeared to be to ask a friend to live along beside me. Karen is silent, discreet, and so sensitive to my inner self, as I hope I am to hers, that I feel sure it will work. We are the same breed of animal and understand each other very well despite the twenty-year difference in our ages.

Saturday, November 3rd

ALREADY THE HOUSE has become a family house, and happiness floods in. Already Karen has transformed the guest room into a room of her own and has begun to work there, and we are coming into a gentle rhythm for the days. She gets up at five and goes back to bed with her tea and I get up around half past six, make my breakfast, and have it on a tray in my bed. Then at eight Karen jumps rope and does yoga exercises in the library, much to Tamas's delight. How invigorating it is to feel someone else working and thinking beside me, a constant transfusion of energy! I realize what a hard lift it has required all these years to have to animate everything alone, and, when there is a guest, to plan things to do. This dear person does not make for extra effort, but just the opposite, reduces the effort, quick to see what needs to be done. And we live along, talking when we feel like it, mostly at supper time. The hazard was that we would feel crowded out of inner space, but my hope that this would not be true has proved right. She will be away for two days a week in Camden and that means a package of solitude every week for me, and a return to her own life and her friends for her. It looks like a fine arrangement, at least until the winter snowstorms begin!

What fun also to be cooking for someone besides myself! We'll take turns, and this first week is my week. It brings back all the things I used to make for Judy, such as eggplant stuffed with chopped ham, mushrooms, and onions which we had last night. I think of us now as Ceres and Persephone, only this Persephone comes in the winter months, not to stay forever, but to come and go as light as air, as warming as sunshine in the bitter cold. Today it is raining and we are going to a movie, and to supper first at a woman's place in Portsmouth called Clarence's Chowder House. I have not been to a movie for months. Peaceful companionship—oh, how blest I am!

Yesterday was warm and blowy, and I went out and did quite a piece of gardening, beginning to clear away the dead stalks of the annuals and putting in three lilies in the back border. Lilies are proving to be very useful flowers for indoors, because they last so long and have such style. I am planting more each year.

Friday, November 9th

I UNEARTHED A RECORD of Casals' playing in the Schubert String Quartet in C Major, such a poignant conversation between the instruments, it fits this gray November day. Now I am reading over the journal and revising I see that I have made a good journey out of depression and rage, and it is time soon to make an end of this means of handling those demons. It has served its purpose.

Reading back I asked myself why when, after all, so many people come and go out of this house, old friends, new friends, friends of the work, loneliness has been one of the recurring themes this year. How can I be lonely when an immense human family surrounds me, bearing gifts, praise, their inmost selves, asking only that I listen and be here?

The loneliness has come because I cannot live with the person I love, and because there is no gentle river of communion that runs along under all the days. Karen's coming here and our perfect accord has solved it for these winter months, at any rate. I hear her typing away downstairs and feel invisibly supported. I go down at the end of the day and find her reading in the cosy room or cooking supper, and feel restored. Everything does not have to be said or experienced in a few hours . . . much can wait for the day when we'll go on a long walk, or light a fire in the library while it snows outside. There is no pressure. Any guest, even a beloved one, creates pressure and takes me away from my work. Because time is short and the visit soon over a lot must be packed in. Now with Karen I can be nonchalant, relaxed, and truly "at home" with a person around who has very quickly become family.

Without serious depression to combat I should never have imagined asking someone to come and live here at my side. I would have been too afraid of losing solitude. So the depression has had one life-enhancing result. It was working with Karen on the video-tape interview that made me trust her, for I saw then how subtly she exercises authority, how gently she moves among other people's tensions. She has to hire the video-tape machinery and on one of the times last spring, poor Ellie, the cameraman, and she struggled for hours because things were not working right. It was enervating and frustrating, for all three of us, but Karen never lost her sense of the human beings involved, as well as the recalcitrant camera and sound recorder and because of her way of being something was salvaged from an exhausting day.

I feel wonderfully happy and at ease with myself these days. And it is good to see that some of my formerly anguished fellow travelers are also out of the woods and back on the road of their real lives. One is a young woman with small children who has written me sometimes of her fatigue and frustration. The other day she wrote,

This summer has focussed my appreciation of the unique advantages of sharing a child's world of infinite discovery. I recall one particular occasion. On the face of it, the situation could hardly have been more depressing. Halfway to a longed for seashore holiday with my parents, aching for the benison of just watching the waves and abandoning anxiety, the car broke down near New York City. While a third attempt was made to repair it I was on my own in a strange town with two travel-weary and hungry young children, walking along a dusty and crowded roadside toward a delicatessen whose existence I had to take on faith. Yet my despair was replaced with wonder while I watched the children. They darted among the weeds discovering goldenrod and curious and lovely seed pods, wild asters and the ferny leaves of yarrow, pebbles speckled like birds' eggs and the hidden doorways of a chipmunk between the golden and mossy green stones of a retaining wall. I realized as I never have before how often we limit our sensory experience by enjoying it only in places we consider appropriate—in carefully preserved parks and secluded forests, on imposing mountains and abandoned stretches of beach. My three-year-old son can see more life in a crack in the sidewalk than I might experience on a guided nature walk. And, happily, he shares it all with me.

For her, as for me, in our very different circumstances, the road has opened by our each accepting what cannot be changed and going with instead of against the current.

Monday, November 12th

LAST NIGHT on "60 Minutes" a wonderful experience was given the audience, to enter a school in the slums of Chicago, run by one black woman for black children ranging in age from five to thirteen. Her name is Marva Collins, and the school the West Side Preparatory School. She had taught in public schools and become disgusted by the plethora of gadgets, tools, gymnasiums, and the lack of real teaching of the fundamentals, especially to read and write, and decided to open up rooms in her own house, one of a row of tall somewhat neglected houses in the area. There she stood, a lean, angular woman with a fiercely intense face, brilliant black eyes, facing a school-room of small black children of whom she demands hard work and no play from eight to three every day, of whom she demands homework, and who are eager to do it, who take books to bed. And what do they read? Who are their favorite authors? When the question was asked by Morley Safer hands went up and the amazing answers were "Chaucer, Shakespeare" from a boy who looked about nine, "Dostoyevsky" from a slightly older boy, and so it went, and it was clear that reading had become the great-est thing in their lives. Later on when parents were inter-viewed some laughed and said they had to take books away from their small children so they could get some sleep! The whole emphasis is on words, language, respect and love of adequate expression, no plea for "Black Eng-lish" here, because, says Miss Miracle, they will not be ready for top jobs unless they can communicate. They are expected to write a short theme every day.

Well, genius is at work in that classroom and genius does not appear every day in the teaching profession. But what it proves is that we are still taking it for granted in public schools that the black students are going to be slow, even retarded. Some of these children had been so bored in the public school they attended before that they were considered unable to learn!

On a rainy dark November evening, that twenty min-utes shone with a brilliant light. I went to bed thinking about it, and thinking how Katharine Taylor would have rejoiced in what we saw were she still alive. That was because I have been reading Ed Yeoman's lucid descrip-tion and analysis of *Shady Hill School, the first fifty years* and Katherine Taylor was principal when I was there as a student. Miss Collins is a kind of Shady Hill School all by herself.

I am the living proof that a good education in the first nine years of one's life is enough if it has taught one how to learn, for after Shady Hill I went on to the Cambridge High and Latin, and that was my whole formal education. At Shady Hill I learned to be wary of facility, learned to dig in to what really mattered to me, and learned where to find the tools and how to use them. And at Shady Hill I was constantly in the presence of people, my teachers, who cared about what was happening in the world and made it quite clear in their own lives and in what they taught us that caring means sharing, sharing not in a glib way but by taking the social problems into the school itself and trying to provide answers there. For example Katharine Taylor started the apprentice teaching plan partly in order to train teachers for Shady Hill but also to send them out into the public schools. Shady Hill began to integrate twenty years ago, and started summer school for deprived children about then.

I cannot imagine what my life would have been without that school and it is with a kind of awe and a great deal of love and gratitude that I copy here some words Katharine Taylor spoke to the parents in 1947:

> For intellectual discipline implies more than obliga-
> tion, obedience, and effort. It reaches a deeper level
> of learning than this. It implies not merely compe-
> tence, but depth of thought. It implies allegiance to
> thought, and response to its demands. It is more con-
> cerned with the process of understanding than with
> haste to use the results, or with personal profit or
> recognition. It carries one through long spells of
> drudgery without the promise of prizes or success. . . .

And unless the students can acquire the discipline which includes selflessness and imagination, how can they perceive and do their part in relation to civilization? This kind of discipline, the fusion of mind and will with the spiritual aims of life, does not develop well in an atmosphere of materialism or inertia or cynicism. Honest uncertainty or scepticism are probably less harmful to it, but it is belief that nourishes it. If we wish to develop it in young people, we must develop it in ourselves. And we must, without arrogance, help them to draw the meaning out of their experience, remembering that it is their meaning, not necessarily identical with ours, that they must find. We must help them to see not only the imperative need, but the keen enjoyment of using one's full will and intelligence, of losing one's self in something beyond one's self, whether it be chemistry research, or poetry, or the furthering of democracy, or international relations, or the endless battle for social justice, or teaching, or the difficult art of intimate daily living with others.

No wonder we, in the ninth grade, wept bitter tears at our desks on "the last day" because it seemed the end of everything and nothing in the future could possibly be as good, as loved and life-enhancing as the Shady Hill School! But what we could not realize fully then was that the school and its standards had been built into us and we would take them on with us through, as in my case, the next fifty years, a firm foundation on which to stand through hell and high water.

November 30th

IN SOME WAYS I am reluctant to come to the end of this journal. There seems always something I want to think about, talk with myself about. I shall miss the daily coming to grips with whatever has been going on. This morning I woke to another radiant day and the large perimeter of dark blue ocean now all the leaves are gone, and watched the sun come up through a wide deep orange band. I lay there trying to find the way through a spell of cold rage into some way of handling it through enlarging its perimeter from the intensely personal into the universal. And I found myself remembering something I was told years ago about an orphanage in Algeria, and how these infants and small children had been in some cases so deprived of love that they had become mentally retarded. The nurses tried to pick them up and cuddle them once or twice a day, but they were so many and the nurses so few that many were expected to grow up half human, their minds affected by lack of touch. Deprivation of any kind makes monsters of us all. But we must regard these monsters with compassion and do all we can, hard as that is when the monsters involved are adults and can hurt us badly, to give them what they sorely need. We cannot withdraw love without damaging ourselves. I have been badly hurt again but I see this morning that it does not really matter because I perceive the truth. Rage is the deprived infant in me but there is also a compassionate mother in me and she will come back with her healing powers in time. In fact if I have learned anything in this year of recovering, that is what I have learned.

I have been reading Peter Matthiessen's remarkable book, *The Snow Leopard,* and laughed with delight at this short passage the other day about the Sherpas.

> Phu-Tsering's awestruck face, so like a child's, reminds me of G. S.'s story of the time in eastern Nepal when our cook received a letter saying that his wife had left him for another man. Weeping, Phu-Tsering had got to his feet and read the letter aloud to all the Sherpa villagers where they were camped, and the people had all stood there and wept with him. As GS commented, "a Westerner would have slunk off and kicked stones; you have to admire the Sherpas for being so open about everything—so open, so without defense, therefore so free, true Bodhisattvas, accepting like the variable airs the large and small events of every day."

Am I a Sherpa at heart?